AF600427

THE JURISDICTION OF THE LATIN ORDINARIES OVER THEIR ORIENTAL SUBJECTS

THE CATHOLIC UNIVERSITY OF AMERICA
CANON LAW STUDIES
No. 229

The Jurisdiction of the Latin Ordinaries Over Their Oriental Subjects

A HISTORICAL SYNOPSIS AND A COMMENTARY

BY THE

REV. MICHAEL FERDINAND DIEDERICHS, J.C.L.
Of the Congregation of the Priests of the Sacred Heart

A DISSERTATION
SUBMITTED TO THE FACULTY OF THE SCHOOL OF CANON LAW OF THE CATHOLIC UNIVERSITY OF AMERICA IN PARTIAL FULFILLMENT OF THE REQUIREMENTS FOR THE DEGREE OF DOCTOR OF CANON LAW

THE CATHOLIC UNIVERSITY OF AMERICA PRESS
WASHINGTON, D. C.
1946

NIHIL OBSTAT:

H. LUDOVICUS MOTRY, S.T.D., J.C.D.
Censor Deputatus
Washingtonii, die 12 februarii, 1947

IMPRIMI POTEST:

GUIL. L. NOLKEN, S.C.J.
Præpositus Provincialis
Hales Corners, Wis., die 14 februarii, 1947

IMPRIMATUR:

✠ MOSES E. KILEY
Archiepiscopus Milwaukiensis
Milwaukiæ, die 17 februarii, 1947

PRINTED IN THE UNITED STATES OF AMERICA
BY THE SERAPHIC PRESS, MILWAUKEE, WIS.

To the
Sacred Heart of Jesus

TABLE OF CONTENTS

Part Two

Canonical Commentary

CHAPTER IV

CHAPTER V

CHAPTER VI

CHAPTER VII

FOREWORD

In the following study the writer attempts to outline the extent and the limitation of the jurisdiction of the Latin ordinaries over their Oriental subjects. In the historical part of this dissertation he offers instances of and references to the exercise of this type of jurisdiction in the past. There has never actually been any attempt made to define exactly how far the jurisdiction of the Latin ordinary extends over his Oriental subjects, or how it is limited by the particular laws of the various Oriental rites. Therefore the writer has attempted to emphasize the principles underlying the exercise of jurisdiction and to apply these principles to the relation of the Latin ordinary to his Oriental subjects, using the Code of Canon Law as a guide.

In his commentary the writer has restricted himself to a study of this jurisdictional relation as in existence in the United States, for which reason also he cites only those norms of the particular laws of the Oriental rites which are represented in the United States.

In several divisions the writer has used the terms *Discipline* and *Rite* as was done in the *Fonti* prepared for the guidance of the scholars occupied with the codification of the Oriental Code. The term *Discipline* is used to indicate only the five major divisions among the Orientals. The term *Rite* is used more indiscriminately, indicating at times a subdivision of one of the five disciplines or a nationality, and at times even pointing to the five disciplines considered as a group if the matter of liturgical unity is to be expressed.

The writer wishes to acknowledge his sincere gratitude to the Congregation of the Priests of the Sacred Heart, to the Very Rev. William L. Nolken, S.C.J., Provincial of the North American Province, for the privilege of advanced study in Canon Law, to the Faculty of the School of Canon Law of the Catholic University of America for their assistance, to various priests, Orientals and Latins, for their aid and encouragement.

PART ONE

Historical Synopsis

CHAPTER I

CANON 9 OF THE IV GENERAL COUNCIL OF THE LATERAN

In treating the jurisdiction of the Latin ordinaries over Oriental subjects one must consider canon 9 of the IV General Council of the Lateran (1215), since its ruling has formed the basis for the exercise of this jurisdiction. The legislative content of this canon was long influential in history, though finally its principle, "the prohibition of two ruling bishops in the same diocese," became obsolete. The reason for the legislation was occasioned by the conquest of Constantinople in 1204, and the subsequent establishment of the Latin Kingdom, in which a Latin hierarchy replaced the deposed Byzantine (schismatical) one.[1]

Canon 9 of the IV General Council of the Lateran sought to provide for people of different rites or languages living in a given diocese. For these people, according to their needs and number, competent men were to be supplied to celebrate the divine sacrifice, to administer the sacraments, and in general to care for their spiritual welfare. Further, if the need arose, then the ordinary of such a diocese was to constitute for these people a vicar who

[1] "Postquam clarissima Bizantii urbs, conjunctis Francorum, Venetorumque armis, expugnata fuit, et Balduinus Flandriæ Comes ibidem Imperator est constitutus, opportunum factu reputatum est, ut Constantinopolitanus Patriarcha Latinus crearetur, ad eamque dignitatem Maurocenus evectus fuit, ac ceteræ deinde minores Imperii urbes, Regiæ civitatis exemplar secutæ, Latinos Episcopos habuerunt. Cum igitur, ut cuique facile est intelligere, hujusmodi Episcoporum subditi magna ex parte Græci essent, ut istorum regimini consuleretur, in Concilio Generali Lateranensi IV. quod sub Innocentio III. celebratum fuit, decretum est, non quidem in una eademque urbe geminos Episcopos esse debere, alterum Græcum, et alterum Latinum, quod monstri simile reputatum fuit; verum ut Episcopus Latinus Græcum Suffraganeum seu Vicarium retineret, qui ex illius præscripto omnia ageret: ... " — Benedictus XIV, *De Synodo Diœcesana* (2 vols., Romæ, 1767), lib. II, cap. XII, n. 4.

was subject to him, but never were two bishops to rule in the same diocese. If anyone as an intruder acted contrary to these provisions, he incurred an excommunication; and if the offending party did not manifest any amendment, he was to be deposed from every ecclesiastical office.[2]

The principle underlying this canon, namely that two bishops were not to rule in the same city, was already mentioned in canon 8 of the I General Council of Nicæa (325).[3] The principle there enunciated was reiterated by canon 9 of the IV General Council of the Lateran with a view to correcting abuses and to preventing their occurrence in the future.[4]

With regard to the statement of the case of people of different rites living in the same diocese, both Hostiensis (+1271)[5] and Ioannes Andreæ (1272-1348)[6] as-

---

[2] "Quoniam in plerisque partibus intra eamdem civitatem atque diœcesim permixti sunt populi diversarum linguarum, habentes sub una fide varios ritus et mores, districte præcipimus, ut pontifices hujusmodi civitatum sive diœcesum provideant viros idoneos, qui secundum diversitates rituum et linguarum divina officia illis celebrent et ecclesiastica sacramenta ministrent, instruendo eos verbo pariter et exemplo. Prohibemus autem omnino, ne una eademque civitas sive diœcesis diversos pontifices habeat, tamquam unum corpus diversa capita, quasi monstrum. Sed si propter prædictas causas urgens necessitas postulaverit, pontifex loci catholicum præsulem nationibus illis conformem provida deliberatione constituat sibi vicarium in prædictis, qui ei per omnia sit obediens et subjectus. Unde si quis aliter se ingesserit, excommunicationis se noverit mucrone percussum, et si nec sic resipuerit ab omni ecclesiastico ministerio deponatur, adhibito, si necesse fuerit, brachio sæculari, ad tantam insolentiam compescendam." — Mansi, *Sacrorum Conciliorum Nova et Amplissima Collectio* (53 vols. in 60, Parisiis, 1901-1927), XXII, 998; c. 14, X, *de officio iudicis ordinarii,* I, 31.

[3] Schroeder, *Disciplinary Decrees of the General Councils* (St. Louis: Herder Book Co., 1937), pp. 34 and 514; Vering, *Lehrbuch des katholischen, orientalischen und protestantischen Kirchenrechts* (3. ed., Freiburg im Breisgau: Herder, 1893), p. 626, 2.

[4] Augustinus, *Antiquæ Decretalium Collectiones Commentariis et Emendationibus Illustratæ. Collectio Quarta Decretalium* (Parisiis, 1621), lib. I, tit. XIII, cap. 2; Gillmann, "Der Kommentar des Vincentius Hispanus zu den Kanones des vierten Laterankonzils," — *Archiv für katholisches Kirchenrecht,* CIX (1929), 229 (hereafter cited *AKKR*).

[5] "Ergo adhuc permixtio toleratur, nihil enim obest saluti credentium." — Hostiensis (Henricus de Segusio), *In Quinque Libros Decretalium Commentaria* (3 vols., Venetiis, 1581), lib. I, tit. 31, cap. 14.

[6] "Rituum varietas nihil obest saluti recte credentium, et in quibus consistant, et differant a moribus." — Ioannes Andreæ, *In Quinque Decretalium Librum Novella Commentaria* (5 vols., Venetiis, 1581), lib. I, tit. 31, n. 14.

serted that a difference of rite existed in the Church, but that it was no obstacle to the attainment of eternal life. They wrote this during a time when hardly any Oriental rite was continually in union with Rome, except the Maronites and Italo-Greeks, since the date for permanent union on the part of most of the rites falls after the sixteenth century.

To administer to the needs of a different rite in a diocese, the canon of the Lateran Council provided that capable men or a vicar be appointed, obedient and subject in all things to the ordinary of the place. As far as this vicar was concerned, Hostiensis rightly maintained that a bishop-vicar was understood.[7]

The sources of later centuries prove that such was also always the case. As to the appointment of this bishop-vicar, the canon seemed to provide that the ordinary in question was to appoint him. Yet, as will be shown later, secular powers influenced the election greatly, and confirmation by the Roman Pontiff was always necessary and was always sought. Attention must also be drawn to the words of the canon: "*Si propter prædictas causas urgens necessitas postulaverit.*"

This ruling explains why many dioceses with subjects of the Oriental rite did not have a special vicar appointed for them, inasmuch as his presence was not deemed necessary if there were only a few persons of a different rite in the diocese. With regard to the consecration of this bishop-vicar, the Glossator in his commentary on this canon stated that he was to be consecrated by his own bishop, whose subject he was, and not by the metropoli-

---

[7] "Ergo intelligo etiam Pontificem, id est, episcopum, alioquin non posset ordines celebrare, non tamen erat èpiscopus istius loci, sed episcopi vicarius . . . sicut parochiani Græci, ita et ipse Græcus sit, et ipsorum ritus servet, qui tamen non sunt per sedem apostolicam reprobati." —Hostiensis, *In Quinque Libros Decretalium Commentaria,* lib. I, tit. 31, cap. 14.

tan.[8] As co-consecrators two neighboring bishops were to be called in.[9]

In order that the provisions of this canon might be properly enforced, an *ipso facto* incurred excommunication was threatened against any intruder who assumed office contrary to the enacted provisions. If an offending cleric proved incorrigible, that is, *crescente contumacia,* as Hostiensis put it, secular aid was to be invoked for his deposition.[10] Subsequent history does not record the incurring of this excommunication on the part of anyone, nor does it recount that secular aid was ever employed to depose any intruding cleric.

Subsequently the continued application of canon 9 of the IV General Council of the Lateran will be illustrated, and thereupon its eventual inoperation will be considered. The purpose of this canon to provide special care for Orientals in a diocese is now reflected in the Code of Canon Law in canon 366, § 3, where it is ruled that only one vicar general should be appointed in a diocese, unless the diversity of rites or the extensive size of the diocese calls for the services of an added vicar general.

---

[8] "Sed a quo consecrabitur iste episcopus? Respondeo, a suo episcopo, non a metropolitano, cum ei non subsit." —*Glossa* in c. 14, X, *de officio iudicis ordinarii,* I, 31.

[9] "Erit autem iste episcopus vicarius et suffraganeus ordinarii, et ab ipso iunctis sibi duobus aliis consecrabitur." —Hostiensis, *In Quinque Libros Decretalium Commentaria,* lib. I, tit. 31, cap. 14.

[10] *Glossa* in c. 14, X, *de officio iudicis ordinarii,* I, 31; Hostiensis, *op. cit.,* lib. I, tit. 31, cap. 14.

CHAPTER II

HISTORY AND LEGISLATION

ARTICLE 1. AMONG THE ITALO-GREEK-ALBANIANS

I. THE ITALO-GREEKS

A. Historical Background

The name Italo-Greeks is used here rather than that of Italo-Albanians, inasmuch as the latter term is now applied exclusively to the Italo-Albanian rite of the Byzantine discipline by the Sacred Congregation for the Oriental Church.[1] The choice of the term Italo-Greeks is likewise more appropriate, since the present article is to treat only the Italo-Greeks of the period prior to the time of the arrival of the Albanians among them in the fifteenth century, which event warranted a change of name for the newly constituted group.

The first traces of Christianity among them are reported in Acts, XXVIII, 11-14. This establishes the faith of the Italo-Greeks as resting upon an Apostolic foundation.[2]

In the earliest centuries Greek was the language commonly used in the Church. In the West, Latin supplanted the Greek as late as the middle of the third cen-

---

[1] S. Congregazione Orientale, *Codificazione Canonica Orientale, Fonti* (3 series, Roma: Tipografia Poliglotta Vaticana, 1930-), Serie I, Fascicolo VIII; hereafter the first series will be cited as *Fonti,* the second series as *Fonti,* Serie II, Fasc., and the third series will be cited unabbreviated; for a complete list of all volumes published up to the present time confer Appendix II; S. Congregazione Orientale, *Statistica con cenni storici della Gerarchia e dei Fedeli di Rito Orientale* (Roma: Tipografia Poliglotta Vaticana, 1932), p. 116 (hereafter cited *Statistica*).

[2] "We set sail after three months in an Alexandrian ship with the Twins on her figurehead, which had wintered at the island [Malta]. We put in at Syracuse, and stayed there three days. Then, following the coast, we reached Rhegium; and one day later a south wind sprang up, and on the second day we arrived at Puteoli, where we found brethren, and were entreated to stay with them seven days; and so we came to Rome." (Taken from the Confraternity edition of the New Testament)

tury. However, in Southern Italy Greek still remained the vernacular tongue, the while Latin was spreading quite influentially in the provinces of the Western Roman Empire. During this time the main Churches had retained their own liturgy. The conquest of Italy during the time of the Emperor Justinian I (527-565) brought the Greeks of Southern Italy again in closer relation with the East. In the eighth century the Iconoclast Emperor Leo III (717-741) subjected Southern Italy, at that time still belonging to the Eastern Empire, to the authority of the Patriarchate of Constantinople, although it had been a Roman ecclesiastical province before the Iconoclast troubles.[3] The Pope could do nothing else but accept the situation. The only Latin element remaining in Southern Italy were the Lombards, who had invaded Italy in 568, spread over the entire peninsula, and had been converted to the Catholic Faith in the sixth and seventh century.

The conquest of Southern Italy and Sicily by the Normans started about the middle of the eleventh century and continued for about another century. It was a momentous factor in the history of the Italo-Greeks, in so far as it brought about their return to the immediate jurisdiction of the Pope, and thus prevented their being drawn into the schism of 1054. On the other hand, the conquest of the Normans and the subsequent increase of the Latin element spelled the gradual disappearance of the Italo-Greeks, until the arrival of the Albanians in the fifteenth century introduced a new Greek element into the dying rite.[4]

---

[3] Fortescue, *The Uniate Eastern Churches* (London: Burns Oates & Washbourne, Ltd., 1923), p. 80.

[4] For further reasons and details see Fortescue, *The Uniate Eastern Churches*, p. 102. The same book also contains an excellent history on the Italo-Greeks and Albanians, pp. 47-145. Also for a more complete history of the Italo-Greeks confer *Fonti*, VIII, 225 ff; *Statistica*, p. 116; Attwater, *The Catholic Eastern Churches* (Milwaukee: The Bruce Publishing Company, 1935), pp. 69-75.

B. *The Jurisdiction of the Latin Ordinary over the Italo-Greeks*

The policy of the Normans was to place the Italo-Greeks in Southern Italy and Sicily under the jurisdiction of the Latin ordinaries as much as this was possible. The power of the Patriarch of Constantinople disappeared with the lost power of the Emperor, and since the Normans did not allow any communication with Constantinople, this factor prevented the extension of the schism of 1054 to the Italo-Greeks, and kept them in communion with Rome.

The first Norman kings subjected especially the Byzantine clergy and even the monasteries under the jurisdiction of the resident Latin ordinaries. Their intermingling in church affairs was based on the treaty made between them and Pope Nicholas II (1059-1061) at the Council of Melfi in 1059.[5] The Council of Melfi had been convoked especially for the purpose of formulating this treaty, and also with a view to restoring ecclesiastical discipline with regard to clerical celibacy. However, no specific legislation for the Italo-Greeks was enacted. In fact, no legislation was made for the Byzantine rite in Southern Italy until the arrival of the Albanians.

In trying to establish a list of the hierarchy who exercised jurisdiction over the Italo-Greeks, one must consider several factors:

1. The Normans, whenever it was possible, tried to have Latin bishops succeed the Byzantine ones.

---

[5] Mansi, *Sacrorum Conciliorum Nova et Amplissima Collectio,* XIX, 919-922; Mercati, *Raccolta di Concordati su Materie ecclesiastiche tra la Santa Sede e le Autorità civili* (Roma: Tipografia Poliglotta Vaticana, 1919), p. 1; Hefele-Leclerq, *Histoire des Conciles* (10 vols. in 19, Paris: Letouzey et Ané, 1907-1938), IV, 1180-1190; Hergenröther, *Handbuch der allgemeinen Kirchengeschichte* (2. ed., 2 vols., Freiburg im Breisgau: Herder, 1879-1880), I, 621.

2. The Byzantine Emperors, while they had power in Southern Italy during the eighth and ninth century, had established two ecclesiastical provinces in Calabria with archbishoprics at Reggio and Santa Severina, and one in Apulia with the metropolitan see at Otranto. For the Lombards in that territory the Popes (Adrian I [772-795], Nicholas I [858-867], and John XIII [965-972]) had set up their own Latin provinces with archbishoprics at Naples, Amalfi, Capua, Benevento, and Salerno.[6]

3. Due to the preponderance of the Roman rite after the Norman conquest, there was naturally a tendency to overwhelm the scattered Byzantine rite.

Following is a list of the hierarchy of Southern Italy and Sicily in relation to the Italo-Greeks till the arrival of the Albanians.

1. Bishoprics with bishops of the Byzantine rite even after the time of the Normans:

Belonging to the Metropolitan see of Reggio:

Bova (Bovensis). It had Byzantine bishops till Julius Staurieno, the first Latin bishop, was appointed by Pius V in 1571.[7] With his arrival the Byzantine rite in this diocese disappeared.

Gerace (Hieracensis). Here the bishops also were of the Byzantine rite till 1467, when Bishop Barlaam turned Latin in opposition to the schismatics of Constantinople, against whom he had vigorously argued at the Council of Florence (1438-1445).[8]

---

[6] Fortescue, *The Uniate Eastern Churches*, pp. 90 ff.

[7] "Hi omnes ritu Græco in sacris usi sunt usque ad Gregorii XIII pontificatum." — Ughelli, *Italia Sacra, sive de Episcopis Italiæ et insularum adiacentium* (2 ed., 10 vols., Venice: Sebastian Coleti, 1721), IX, 339 (hereafter cited *Italia Sacra*); Fortescue, *The Uniate Eastern Churches*, p. 109.

[8] "Episcopus Hieracensis autem Græci quondam ritus et obedientiæ fuit usque ad annum Dom. 1467, quo abdicatis Græcorum ritibus, Romanæ Ecclesiæ cœremonias cœpit . . ." — Ughelli, *Italia Sacra*, IX, 393; Fortescue, *The Uniate Eastern Churches*, p. 108.

Oppido (Oppidensis). The Byzantine rite with its own bishop lasted here till the fifteenth century.[9]

The Metropolis *Santa Severina* had Byzantine archbishops. The exact time of the change to a Latin metropolitan is unknown. Some writers point to a century as early as the thirteenth, others to a century as late as the sixteenth.[10] After the change, however, the see of Santa Severina was ruled by Latin ordinaries, who had the faithful of the Byzantine rite under their jurisdiction.

Palermo (Panormitanus). This see had Byzantine archbishops during the time of the Normans.[11]

Rossano (Rossanensis) had a Greek bishop till 1460, when a Latin archbishop was installed.[12]

2. Bishoprics, originally Greek, but which during the time of the Normans received Latin Ordinaries:

Belonging to the Metropolitan see of Reggio:

Reggio (Rhegiensis) itself, previously of the Byzantine rite, was changed to the Roman rite by Roger I of Sicily (1071-1101) in 1081, which act was confirmed by Gregory VII (1073-1085).[13]

Catanzaro (Catacensis). This bishopric, struggling for its very existence as long as it had Greek bishops, turned Latin under Paschal II (1107), when it also started to flourish with renewed life and vigor.[14]

Croto (Crotonensis). Of this diocese it is known that its Greek Bishop Philip attended the III General Council

---

[9] "Episcopatus Oppidensis Græcus olim fuit . . ." — Ughelli, *Italia Sacra*, IX, 417; Fortescue, *The Uniate Eastern Churches*, p. 108.

[10] Fortescue, *op. cit.*, p. 97.

[11] Fortescue, *op. cit.*, p. 98. The writer was not able to find any further information in this regard.

[12] Ughelli, *Italia Sacra*, IX, 307; Gams, *Series Episcoporum Ecclesiæ Catholicæ* (Ratisbonæ, 1873), p. 917.

[13] Fortescue, *The Uniate Eastern Churches*, p. 98.

[14] Ughelli, *Italia Sacra*, IX, 355 ff.

of the Lateran in 1179, but the later bishops seem to have been Latin.[15]

Tropea (Tropeiensis) furnishes a typical example of the Norman policy, as Roger I skillfully maneuvered it into the Latin rite in the year 1094.[16]

Squillace (Squillacensis vel Scyllacensis) was tactfully turned over to the Latin rite by Roger I upon the death of its Byzantine Bishop Theodor Mesmer with the help of the Bishop of Santa Severina.[17]

Belonging to the Metropolitan See of Otranto:

The Metropolis *Otranto* (Hydruntinus), itself once Greek, turned Latin in the eleventh century[18] as did also its suffragan sees *Alessano* (Alexanensis)[19] and *Ugento* (Uxentinus).[20] Regarding the status of its suffragan see of Gallipoli special mention will follow later.

Mention may here be made of the old see of St. Leo as having formerly had Greek bishops. It received Latin prelates on its subjection to the Metropolitan See of Santa Severina.[21]

---

[15] "Philippus Græcus Episcopus Crotonensis interfuit Lateranensi Concilio sub Alexandro III anno 1179." — Ughelli, *Italia Sacra,* IX, 384; Fortescue, *op. cit.,* p. 99.

[16] "Græcus fuit episcopatus Tropeiensis ad annum usque 1094, quo Rogerius Apuliæ, Calabriæ et Siciliæ Dux, constituto primo ex Latinis episcopo Iustego nobili Tropeam ecclesiam exornavit privilegio." — Ughelli, *Italia Sacra,* IX, 449; Fortescue, *The Uniate Eastern Churches,* p. 98.

[17] "Ioannes de Nicephoro Canonicus et Decanus Militensis ecclesiæ electus est huius ecclesiæ primus Latinorum Episcopus anno 1096 . . ." —Ughelli, *Italia Sacra,* IX, 426; "Stephanus Episcopus S. Severinæ memoratur in charta Rogerii Comitis anno 1096 pro constituendo Episcopo Latini ritus in ecclesia et civitate Squillacensi." — Ughelli, *Italia Sacra,* IX, 475; Fortescue, *The Uniate Eastern Churches,* p. 98.

[18] Ughelli, *Italia Sacra,* IX, 51-67; Fortescue, *op. cit.,* p. 98.

[19] ". . . a Græcis Episcopis diu administratus fuit: quibus pulsis, Latinus episcopus a Romanis Pontificibus constitutus . . ." Ughelli, *Italia Sacra,* IX, 87.

[20] ". . . urgentibus episcopis ad Latinam normam conversæ sunt . . ." — Ughelli, *Italia Sacra,* IX, 110.

[21] "Antiquitus Græcum habet episcopum, deinde posterioribus sæculis Latinum Metropoli S. Severinæ subiectum." — Ughelli, *Italia Sacra,* IX, 513. Pius V in 1571 suppressed this bishopric and united it with Santa Severina.

3. Bishoprics, Latin in their origin, but having subjects of the Byzantine rite:

In the province of Reggio, aside from what has been said of Reggio itself, the Byzantine rite existed also at *Cassana* (Cassanensis)[22] and *Nicastro* (Neocastrensis).[23]

In the Archdiocese of *Brindisi* there existed some Greeks during the time of the Normans. In the suffragan diocese of Nardo, abolished by Pope Paul I (757-767) in 761, but restored again by Pope Gregory XII (1406-1415) in 1413, the Byzantine rite was predominant. Fortescue (1874-1923) mentions also that the Archbishop of Brindisi appointed an archpriest *(Protopapa)* for this rite in Nardo.[24]

Lecce (Lyciensis), a suffragan of Otranto, had members of the Byzantine rite.[25]

At Rivello in the diocese of *Policastro* (Policastrensis), which was a suffragan of Salerno, there were two parishes, one for the Latins and one for the Greeks.[26]

The Archbishopric of *Taranto* (Tarentinus) had some subjects of the Byzantine rite.[27]

In the Archbishopric of Naples there were some Byzantine parishes in the thirteenth century.[28]

On the Island of Sicily, besides what has been mentioned about Palermo, the sees of Syracuse, Messina, and Troina also had members of the Byzantine rite.[29]

---

[22] Ughelli, *Italia Sacra,* IX, 343.

[23] Ughelli, *Italia Sacra,* IX, 401.

[24] *The Uniate Eastern Churches,* p. 112.

[25] "... est quidem Ecclesia Græcorum, in qua Græcus Parochus quadraginta eius Nationis familiis Catholico Græcorum more et ritus administrat." — Ughelli, *Italia Sacra,* IX, 68.

[26] "... alterum (oppidum) est Rivellum duas habens parochiales, quorum in una Latinus Archipresbyter Latino, in altera Græcus, populo Græco suis cum clericis sacra, suæ gentis more administrat ..." — Ughelli, *Italia Sacra,* VII, 542.

[27] Ughelli, *Italia Sacra,* IX, 120; Fortescue, *The Uniate Eastern Churches,* p. 114.

[28] Fortescue, *op. cit.,* p. 99.

[29] Fortescue, *op. cit.,* p. 100. The text of Fortescue erroneously lists the diocese as Traina.

Finally, an exceptional case in relation to the foregoing classification deserves specific mention here. *Gallipoli* (Gallipolitanus), a suffragan see of Otranto, had alternately Byzantine and Roman bishops till the fourteenth century.[30]

C. The "Protopapa" of the Italo-Greeks under the Latin Bishop

The Latin ordinaries administered the needs of the Italo-Greeks subject to them with no marked difference from the way in which they administered the affairs of their Latin subjects. The Italo-Greeks, however, used the Byzantine rite in their Liturgy, for no special legislation for them was then as yet in existence.

The theory that the *Archipresbyter* or the Greek *Protopapa* was the instrument used by the Latin bishops to administer that part of their flock which was of the Byzantine rite holds good only insofar as the *Protopapa* directed the clergy and faithful in his own district, that is, where he was stationed. As proof for this theory the fact is proposed that there were several *Protopapæ* in a diocese which had members of the Byzantine rite, and not simply one who had jurisdiction over all the members of the Byzantine rite. Fortescue cites several instances to this effect.[31]

---

[30] "Accedit huic sententiæ, quod Ecclesia Gallipolitana tanquam a posterioribus colonis Græcis etiamnunc instituta, ritusque Græcorum obtinet, quodque in more habebat nunc originis, gentisque Græcanicæ [sic] nunc Latinæ, per vices Episcopum creare." — Ughelli, *Italia Sacra,* IX, 98; Fortescue, *The Uniate Eastern Churches,* p. 112.

[31] ". . . at Gerace two Greek canons, four Protopapæ; . . . at Catanzaro . . . three Protopapæ. At Nicastro two Protopapæ . . . At Squillace . . . four Protopapæ . . ." — Fortescue, *The Uniate Eastern Churches,* p. 100. On page 106 the same author states: "Joseph Morisani, Canon of Reggio, wrote a whole book about them (protopapæ) 'De Protopapis et Deutereis Græcorum et Catholicis eorum ecclesiis Diatriba.' (Naples, 1769). In this he traces the history and the meaning of the titles and gives much valuable information about the Italo-Greeks in general." The writer regrets that this book was not available to him. The theory proposed above might well be even more strongly confirmed through additional information on that subject.

However, Fortescue mentions also two other instances. The *Protopapa* of Reggio had quasi-episcopal jurisdiction over all of the Byzantine rite in the Archdiocese.[32] The *Protopapa* at Nardo had been appointed by the Archbishop of Brindisi at the time when the Diocese of Nardo was united with the Archbishopric of Brindisi.[33]

These two instances, however, do not contradict the theory proposed above, but rather confirm it. For the *Protopapa* of Reggio had these special and unique powers over the members of his rite throughout the diocese, not by common law or custom, but by privilege.[34] The *Protopapa* at Nardo in the Archdiocese of Brindisi was in reality only a *Protopapa* over a district, as was usually the case. For he was appointed by the Archbishop of Brindisi, not for the Byzantine rite in the Archdiocese, for that rite was dying out there, and hence no *Protopapa* was needed, but rather for the suppressed Diocese of Nardo, which had a greater number of the Byzantine rite. Accordingly, he was appointed for the district of Nardo.

Canon 9 of the IV General Council of the Lateran (1215), which proposed a vicar for a different rite in a given diocese, was not applied during the thirteenth and fourteenth century in Southern Italy and Sicily, since the Byzantine rite was dying out in the dioceses which had a Latin ordinary and Italo-Greek subjects.

II. THE ITALO-ALBANIANS

The fall of Constantinople in 1453 to the Turks together with the subsequent invasion of the Balkans had

---

[32] Fortescue, *op. cit.*, p. 106.

[33] Fortescue, *op. cit.*, p. 112.

[34] "Le Comte Roger Ier donna aux Grecs la grande et célebre église de Notre-Dame à Reggio, il y établit un protoprêtre pour lequel il obtint du Pape les droits d'Archimandrite d'un convent stavropigiaque. Ce privilège de l'indépendance du protoprêtre de cette église vis-à-vis de tout évêque fut maintenu jusqu'en 1611." — Pierre, "L'union de l'Orient avec Rome." — *Orientalia Christiana*, XVIII (1930), 111.

already caused a number of Christians to seek refuge in the West. Among these were the Albanians who professed to be Uniates of the Byzantine rite. They were the first ones to stimulate the growth in numbers among the diminishing Italo-Greeks. However, the main stream of Albanians from the Balkans started to arrive after 1467, and their immigration into Italy continued for the next one hundred years. This arrival as late as 1467 seems explained by the fact that George Alexander Castriota (Scanderbeg) had succeeded in establishing the independence of the Albanians from the Turks, which status lasted till his death in 1468.

During his lifetime Scanderbeg had established friendly relations with the Pope and with Italian princes, especially the King of Naples. So after the death of Scanderbeg, when the persecution of Christians by the Turks began, the Albanians fled to the nearest haven of safety, which was Italy, settling especially in the southern part and in Sicily, though a small number of them went to other parts of Italy, such as Venice. Though there were among these refugees some schismatics, the greater part of them maintained that they were Catholics in union with Rome, and that they were of the Greek rite within the Byzantine discipline. These really were the ones whose presence assured the continuance of the Byzantine rite in Southern Italy, when the Italo-Greeks were dying out. Accordingly, from that time on the members of the Byzantine rite in Southern Italy and Sicily are more correctly called the Italo-Albanians.

It is but natural that many difficulties should arise upon the arrival and the settlement of the Albanians in Italy and Sicily. Disputes arose especially when they began to claim exemption from the jurisdiction of the Latin ordinaries, and when wandering bishops of the Byzantine rite began to exercise jurisdiction over the Albanians much to the dismay of the local Latin ordinaries.[35] Though the stream of papal constitutions proves on the one hand the disorders and difficulties that had arisen, their issuance in such numbers on the other hand was a sign of the continuous papal solicitude to rectify matters, to counsel, and to give the needed directions.

On June 3, 1514, Leo X (1513-1521) issued the Constitution *Pro parte vestra* to the Albanian community which had established itself at Venice.[36] The Constitution provided for this community a priest of the Byzantine rite to care for it and to administer to its needs according to their rite. It exempted him from the local Latin ordinary, and subjected him immediately to the Holy See. On May 18, 1521, Leo X in his Constitution *Accepimus nuper* provided regulations for the affairs between the Latins and the Greeks.[37] This Constitution was followed on July 4 in the same year with the Constitution *Cum nuper,* which established a commission for solving the difficulties and abuses.[38]

Paul III (1534-1549) in his Constitution *Dudum* of December 23, 1534, stated that the Greeks were to observe all things decreed by the previous Pontiffs.[39] He provided that, wherever there were any Greek bishops, they were to exercise jurisdiction over the Greeks, and the Latin bishops jurisdiction over the Latins. In his Constitution *Dudum postquam* of June 22, 1549, the same Pope confirmed the privileges granted by Leo X for the Greeks at Venice.[40]

Yet, inasmuch as the Greeks under the pretext of im-

---

[35] Fortescue, *The Uniate Eastern Churches,* p. 120.

[36] *Appendix ad Bullarium Pontificium S. Congregationis de Propaganda Fide* (2 vols., Romæ: Typis Collegii Urbani [no date given]), I, 14-15 (hereafter cited *Appendix ad Bullarium S. C. de Prop. Fide); Fonti,* VIII, 242.

[37] Allatius, *De Aetate et Interstitiis in collatione Ordinum etiam apud Græcos servandis* (Romæ: Mascardus, 1638), pp. 5-13; *Fonti,* VIII, 242.

[38] *Appendix ad Bullarium S. C. de Prop. Fide,* I, 17-19; *Fonti,* VIII, 243.

[39] *Appendix ad Bullarium S. C. de Prop. Fide,* I, 21-24.

[40] *Appendix ad Bullarium S. C. de Prop. Fide,* I, 32-36; *Fonti,* VIII, 243.

munities and privileges allegedly granted by various Popes declared themselves exempt from the jurisdiction of the local ordinaries, and also inasmuch as they had fallen into errors, Pius IV (1559-1564) issued his Constitution *Romanus Pontifex* on February 16, 1564, in which he tried to settle the problems between the Greeks and the Latins once for all.[41] He revoked all privileges that had been granted to them. Then he definitely stated that the Albanians were subject to the visitation, correction, penalties, and jurisdiction of the local ordinaries, who were to see to their general welfare of soul, to the administration of the sacraments, and to the extirpation of heresy. However, the Italo-Albanians were to follow their rite in the celebration of divine services.

On August 31, 1595, Clement VIII (1592-1605) issued his Instruction *Sanctissimus,* directing it to the Latin bishops as a guide in their dealings with the Greeks, especially regarding the administration of the sacraments. In paragraph 7 of this *Instructio Clementina* provision was made for the maintenance at Rome of an ordaining bishop of the Byzantine rite for Italy and its adjacent islands.[42]

The final establishment of norms governing the Italo-Albanians was made by Benedict XIV (1740-1758), when on May 26, 1742, he issued the Constitution *Etsi pastoralis,* which may well be regarded as the particular law of the Italo-Albanians. After treating matters of Faith and of the Sacraments, he added a special paragraph on interritual

---

[41] *Bullarium Pontificium S. Congregationis de Propaganda Fide* (7 vols., Romæ: Typis Collegii Urbani, 1839-1858), I, 8-10 (hereafter cited *Bullarium Pontificium S. C. de Prop. Fide*); *Bullarum Diplomatum et Privilegiorum S. R. Pontificum Taurinensis Editio* (20 vols., Augustæ Taurinorum, 1857-1872; 5 vols., Neapoli, 1867-1885), VII, 271; *Fonti,* VIII, 271; Hergenröther, "Die Rechtsverhältnisse der verschiedenen Riten innerhalb der katholischen Kirche." — *AKKR,* VII (1862), 355.

[42] *Codicis Iuris Canonici Fontes, cura Emi Petri Gasparri editi* (9 vols., Romæ [postea Civitate Vaticana]: Typis Polyglottis Vaticanis, 1923-1939; Vols. VII-IX, ed. cura et studio Emi Iustiniani Card. Serédi), n. 179; *Bullarium Pontificium S. C. de Prop. Fide,* I, 1-4; *Fonti,* VIII, 245-250.

law regulating the extent of the jurisdiction of the local Latin ordinaries over the Italo-Albanians.[48]

Aside from the fact that the Italo-Albanians were to follow their own laws and rite, in several things they were to follow the Latins, namely, in the things to which all the faithful of a diocese without any distinction of persons or rite were obliged. Thus the Italo-Albanians were to follow the Latins in the observance of the Gregorian calendar, and to commemorate the Roman Pontiff and the local ordinary at their divine services. They also were subject to the law as enacted in the papal constitutions *contra sollicitantes*.

The Italo-Albanians dwelling in Latin territories had to observe all the feasts of precept as established in that region. If an entire community of Italo-Albanians could be induced to follow the fasts, abstinences and vigils of the Latins, then it was the Pope's desire that this be accomplished; yet, they were not to be forced to this, and therefore could continue the observance of fasting according to the prescriptions of their own rite. The execution of this matter thus was left to the prudent judgment of the local ordinary.

The Italo-Albanians were to receive their ministrations from the priests of their own rite, and Latin priests were not to mingle with the Greek priests during sacred functions, except when they were especially called for this purpose by the Greeks. On the other hand, Greek priests were not to celebrate sacred functions in Latin churches, except with the special permission of the local Latin ordinary, which permission the ordinary could grant if otherwise the spiritual needs of the Greeks would not have been properly cared for.

---

[48] § 9: "Ritus græcus qua ratione in Italia et insulis adiacentibus servandus: de græcorum seu albanensium subiectione Episcoporum latinorum iurisdictioni," — *Fontes*, n. 328; *Fonti*, VIII, 257, 262.

With regard to the question of precedence among the Latins and Greeks at solemn functions, custom and ecclesiastical dignity were the deciding factors, apart from any comparison that would favor the one or the other rite. The Greeks were to use those liturgical books which had been corrected by the Holy See, and purged by it of all previously retained errors.

Italo-Albanians who did not have a bishop of their own were subject to the local Latin ordinaries, inclusive also of the religious of that rite. When there were two bishops in the same see, one for the Greeks and one for the Latins as appointed by the Holy See, then each one was to care for the flock belonging to his own rite; but if there was but a Latin ordinary in a diocese wherein Greek subjects were resident, then a Greek vicar was to take care of all matters concerning their rite. In the case of an appeal to a metropolitan who was a Latin, a Greek judge was to be delegated to expedite the judicial matter. While along with the rest of the faithful the Greek monks likewise were subject to the local Latin ordinaries, they nevertheless were acknowledged to retain intact all the privileges granted them by the previous Popes.[44]

In 1919 the Diocese of Lungro was established for all the Italo-Albanians of the province of Calabria. Those in Sicily continued subject to the Latin ordinaries with an ordaining bishop at Palermo. They number about 50,000 altogether. In the United States they have in New York City one church which is subject to the local Latin ordinary. At present and since 1930 the Italo-Albanians in Southern Italy, i.e., those who belong to the Diocese of

---

[44] *Fontes*, n. 328; *Fonti*, VIII, 257-262; Hergenröther, "Die Rechtsverhältnisse der verschiedenen Riten innerhalb der katholischen Kirche." — *AKKR*, VII (1862), 255-257; Arndt, "Die gegenseitigen Rechtsverhältnisse der Riten in der katholischen Kirche." — *AKKR*, LXXI (1894), 234-235; Silbernagel, *Verfassung und gegenwärtiger Bestand sämtlicher Kirchen des Orients* (2 ed., by Joseph Schnitzer, Regensburg, 1904), pp. 325-327.

Lungro (Oriental rite) and also those who reside in Sicily follow the legislation of the Code of Canon Law concerning marriage; for the Ordinary of the Diocese of Lungro and the Ordinaries (Latin rite) of Palermo and Monreale upon asking the Holy Father for this concession in 1930 had it granted to them.[45] However, for the Italo-Albanians living in the United States the Constitution *Etsi pastoralis* still continues as the binding law.[46]

Article 2. Instances of Jurisdiction of Latin Ordinaries Over Orientals Resulting From the Crusades

A result of the first Crusade (1096-1099) was the founding of Edessa, Antioch, and Jerusalem as kingdoms which existed under Western rulers until the time of their

---

[45] This is based on private information received by Dr. Plöchl of the Catholic University of America, Washington, D. C., from Dr. Herman, S.J., consultor of the Sacred Congregation for the Oriental Church. The information in question is hereby verbatim reproduced:

"Was die Italo-Albanesen angeht, so hatten sich die Bischöfe von Lungro (orient. Ritus), Palermo und Monreale an den Hl. Stuhl gewandt und die anderen, auf Anfrage, hatten sich ihnen angeschlossen, mit der Erklärung, dass die Italo-Albanesen seit der Errichtung der Diözese Lungro, bzw. seit der Veröffentlichung des Codex sich im Eherecht immer an das lateinische Eherecht angeschlossen hätten. Die Folge sei aber, dass vielleicht einige Ehen ungültig geschlossen seien. Denn die Ehehindernisse, die seit der Constitution "*Etsi pastoralis*" bei den Italo-Albanesen in Geltung standen, dehnen sich weiter aus als die des Codex; die Verwandtschaft ist Ehehindernis im 4., die Schwägerschaft im 3. und 4. Grad.

"Die beiden Erzbischöfe und der Bischof von Lungro 'hanno perciò rivolta domanda al S. Padre perchè voglia sanare per il passato e per l'avvenire sia data facoltà di appicare agli italo-greci, per la celebrazione del matrimonio, le disposizioni del Codice di Diritto Canonico, almeno interim, usque ad codificationem Can. Orientalem. I pæsi con popolazione di rito orientale si sono infatti adattati volentieri alle norme latine, e volendo introdurre ora quelle del rito bizantino, oltre che alla confusione che accompagnerebbe il capivolgimento dello stato attuale delle cose, ci si troverebbe di fronte a difficoltà di determinare esattamente le norme bizantine e di doverne escludere alcune, non più consone all'indole dei tempi.

" '*Quatenus affirmative,* basterà communicare ciò ai tre Ordinari, senza pubblicarlo negli Acta A. S.?'

"In der Audienz vom 22 Juni 1930 billigte der Hl. Vater die Antwort: 'affirmative quoad sanationem et in posterum usque ad codificationem.' "

[46] Cf. Plöchl, "Two hundred years — *Etsi pastoralis,*" — *The Jurist*, II (1942), 211-213.

reconquest by the Saracens. As the Crusaders moved into Palestine the Greek hierarchy (schismatical since 1054) was disorganized. Upon its flight from the country a Latin hierarchy took its place.[47] However, since the conquest of Palestine by the Crusaders was only of a short duration, many sees were never occupied by the Latin bishops, and some only for a short time. Some of the most noteworthy of these sees were Jerusalem, Cæsarea, Edessa, Antioch, and Laodicea.[48]

The establishment of the Latin Empire of Constantinople was the result of the fourth Crusade (1202-1204): Again with the arrival of the Latins the Greek hierarchy fled, the Patriarch of Constantinople to Nicæa, the court of the Greek Emperor Theodor I Laskaris (1204-1222). The Greeks themselves remained mostly in schism. In fact, not one of the Greek bishops lent his hand to a union with the Latins, which Innocent III (1178-1216) had hoped for and attempted again and again to achieve. However, the political subjection of the Greeks did not imply at the same time an ecclesiastical one. Occupation by the Latins did not imply a union between them and the Greeks.[49]

The Patriarchate of Constantinople comprised twenty-two archbishoprics, yet the Latins actually never conquered the entire country, and therefore not all the former sees under Constantinople came into the hands of the Latins. Gams (1816-1892) restricts his record to Latin bishops who at least for some time took possession of their

---

[47] "Au momet où les croisés sont entrés en Palestine la hiérarchie greque était désorganisée et le patriarche grec s'était réfugié dans l'île de Chypre. Des clercs de rit latin furent donc tout naturellement placés à tous les degrés de la hiérarchie." — Bréhier, *L'église et l'orient au moyen âge, les croisades* (Paris, 1907), p. 92.

[48] Cf. Gams, *Series Episcoporum Ecclesiæ Catholicæ.*

[49] Norden, *Das Papstum und Byzanz* (Berlin, 1903), p. 181; cf. also Rattinger, "Der Patriarchat und Metropolitansprengel von Constantinopel und die bulgarische Kirche zur Zeit der Lateinerherrschaft in Byzanz," — *Görres Gesellschaft: Historisches Jahrbuch,* I (1880), 77.

Greek dioceses; in all he lists fifty-four sees which at one time or another had a Latin bishop ruling over the Orientals.[50]

The history of the origin of the Latin hierarchy on the Island of Cyprus is a stormy one. The Latin hierarchy was introduced by Richard, the Lionhearted (1189-1199), during the third Crusade in 1191. He first of all transferred the Metropolitan see from Salamis (Constantia) to Nikosia and established suffragans at Limasol, Paphos, and Famagusta. These acts were confirmed by Pope Celestine III (1191-1198) in 1196.[51]

But he also established a Latin hierarchy on Cyprus. This action brought about a conflict, since the Latin as well as the Greek hierarchy wanted the ruling power. Till after the IV General Council of the Lateran (1215) the original Greek hierarchy prevailed. But upon the death of the Greek Metropolitan at Nikosia, a Latin Archbishop took over the see, after a newly proposed Greek Archbishop Neophytus had been ousted and thereupon fled to Greece. From then on the Latin hierarchy had the controlling power. It accordingly utilized the ruling of canon 9 of the IV General Council of the Lateran. This implied that the Greek bishops who had jurisdiction over their rite had to obey the Latin bishops, which fact was also confirmed by Pope Honorius III (1216-1227) in 1221.[52]

---

[50] "Cæteros episcopos latinos hic recensere supersedemus, quia vix unus vel alter brevissimum tempus episcopatum suum visitavit." — Gams, *Series Episcoporum Ecclesiæ Catholicæ*, p. 432 ff.

[51] Ecclesiæ Nicosiensis patrocinium suscipit ac possessiones confirmat, eique Paphensem, Limiconiensem et Famagustanum episcopatus subiicit. Alano archiepiscopo eiusque successoribus usum pallii crucisque præferendæ et alia privilegia concedit." —Jaffé, *Regesta Pontificum Romanorum* (2. ed., 2 vols. in 1, Lipsiæ, 1885-1888), n. 17461 (hereafter cited *Jaffé*).

[52] "Confirmatio concordiæ inter Cypri regimen et prælatos eiusdem regni quodque Græci in locis ritus Latini degentes suos episcopos habere minime possint, Latinis tamen subesse teneantur episcopis." — *Bullarum Diplomatum et Privilegiorum S. R. Pontificum*

The Greek bishops who had been reduced to four, equal in number to the Latin bishops, applied to Pope Innocent IV (1243-1254) for a new Archbishop, who was granted to them in 1251.[53] Innocent IV in his Epistle *Sub catholicæ,* issued on March 6, 1254, for Cyprus, upheld his earlier policy when he insisted that the Greeks were not to be molested.[54]

Alexander IV (1254-1261) tried to settle the strife in 1260, when he recognized the previous arrangement of having four Greek bishops along with the four Latin ones, with the Greek bishops subject to the Latin ordinaries according to canon 9 of the IV General Council of the Lateran.[55]

The Turks occupied the Island of Cyprus in 1570, whereupon the Greeks promptly elected for themselves a schismatical metropolitan.

Article 3. In the Austrian Monarchy

The jurisdiction of Latin ordinaries over Orientals as decreed in canon 9 of the IV General Council of the Lateran was exercised through an Oriental bishop-vicar given to the Latin bishops. This manner of exercising jurisdiction was especially in use in the Austrian Monarchy during the eighteenth century, although already in 1234, for a short duration of union with Rome, Gregory IX (1227-1241) in a letter addressed to King Béla IV (1235-1270)

Taurinensis Editio, III, 282; cf. Mansi, *Sacrorum Conciliorum Nova et Amplissima Collectio,* XXII, 1076 and 1084; Pressuti, *Regesta Honorii Papæ III* (2 vols., Romæ: Ex Typographia Vaticana, 1888-1895), n. 3663.

[53] "Episcopis Græcis Cypri concedit, ut in metropolitana sua Archiepiscopo iampridem defuncto alium subrogent." — Potthast, *Regesta Pontificum Romanorum inde ab anno post Christum natum 1198 ad annum 1304* (2 vols., Berolini, 1874-1875), n. 14445; Berger, *Les Registres d'Innocent IV* (4 vols., Paris: Ernst Thorin, 1884-1897), n. 5523.

[54] *Fontes,* n. 34.

[55] Potthast, *Regesta Pontificum Romanorum,* n. 17910; *Fonti,* VIII, 238.

of Hungary stated that the *Episcopi Latini Cumanorum* were to constitute an episcopal vicar for the Wallachians and Rumanians.[56] However, it was not until after the Turks were driven out of Eastern Europe (1683), and a permanent union was established with the Orientals living there, that canon 9 of the IV General Council of the Lateran was consistently applied. But even this policy later fell into disuse during the reign of Emperor Joseph II (1765-1790).

On May 30, 1688, Leopold I (1658-1705) had Longin Raič (Raisch) appointed as Oriental bishop-vicar to the Latin ordinary of Syrmium (Mitrovica) to administer to the Wallachians living there.[57] In 1748 Benedict XIV (1740-1758) in his Letter *Etsi ipsa* of August 30, appointed a bishop-vicar to the Latin Ordinary of Oradea Mare (Grosswardein or Nogyvárod).[58] Similarly all bishop-vicars appointed for Orientals living among Latins and in their dioceses had only a restricted jurisdiction. However, even during this time the Holy See established for the Oriental Rumanians a new bishopric at Fogaras, when it already existed as a Latin see. It was Innocent XIII (1721-1724) who did this in his Bull *Ratione congruit* of

---

[56] So to be found in *Fonti*, VIII, 488 and *Fonti*, X, n. 1219.

[57] Fiedler, "Die Union der in Ungarn zwischen der Donau wohnenden Bekenner des grieschisch-orientalischen Glaubens," — *Sitzungsberichte der philosophisch-historischen Classe der kaiserlichen Akademie der Wissenschaften*, XXXVIII (1862), 284 (hereafter cited Fiedler, *SB*); Plöchl, "Church Laws for Orientals of the Austrian Monarchy in 'the Age of Enlightenment,' " — *Bulletin of the Polish Institute of Arts and Sciences in America*, II (1944), 718 (hereafter cited Plöchl, *Polish Institute*.)

[58] "Deputandum esse Episcopum Suffraganeum, seu Vicarium, Reverendum Meletium Ritus Græci ad formam Canonis IX Concilii Lateranensis IV seu Capituli *Quoniam, de officio Iudicis Ordinarii*, cum dispensatione super irregularitate ob schismata et hæresim incursa, necnon cum assignatione tituli Episcopalis, et congruæ pro eius substentatione in florenis mille et quingentis illarum partium super fructibus mensæ Episcopalis Varadinensis." — Benedictus XIV, *De Synodo Diœcesana*, lib. II, cap. XII, n. 5; *Fonti*, VIII, 517; Hergenröther, "Die Rechtsverhältnisse der verschiedenen Riten innerhalb der katholischen Kirche," — *AKKR*, VII (1862), 257; Plöchl, *Polish Institute*, II (1944), 741.

May 18, 1721, by which he erected the see of Fogaras, and exempted it from any other jurisdiction.[59]

Though it had always been the desire of the Austrian Emperors to have Catholic Oriental bishops as ordinaries *pleno iure,* it was only during the reign of Joseph II that this was successfully accomplished. This question arose and came to a point over the proposed establishment of the diocese of Munkács for the Oriental Church of Podcarpathia. To the petition of Maria Theresa for a Greek bishop in this diocese Pope Clement XIII (1758-1769) replied in the negative in his Letter *Magno cum animi* of July 13, 1768. In declining the request the Pope based his refusal on canon 9 of the IV General Council of the Lateran.[60] However, Clement XIV (1769-1774) revised this decision of his predecessor when he established the Greek diocese of Munkács through his Decree of erection *Eximia regalium,* of September 19, 1771.[61]

---

[59] "... et ut novus Grex Dominicus huiusmodi eorum propriam Sedem, propriumque haberent Pastorem ... a quacumque alia Ordinaria iurisdictione divisit, et separavit, illaque omnia et Clerum ac Populum Ritus huiusmodi, quoad legem Diœcesanam, ab Episcopi Latini Transylvaniensium Superioritate, Jurisdictione, Potestate, Subiectione, Visitatione, et Correctione, si qua in eos consueverat prorsus eximit et liberavit, ac Oppidum Fogarasiense præactatum [sic] in Civitatem erexit, illiusque incolas Civium nomine, titulo et honore decoravit, illudque et in eo Ecclesiam Divo Nicola dicatam in Cathedralem Ritus Græci præfati, ... pro uno Episcopo Ritus Græci redigi faceret, nec non Episcopalem Iurisdictionem, auctoritatem in omnes et singulos Græcos, Ruthenos, Valachos, et Rascianos præfatos, tunc, et pro tempore in universa Provincia præa[c]tata commorantes et commoraturos exercere, omniaque, et singula, quæ Iurisdictionis, quodque Ordinis, et cuiuslibet muneris Episcopalis erant." — *Appendix ad Bullarium S. C. de Prop. Fide,* II, 3-4; *Fonti,* VIII, 504; Nilles, *Symbolæ ad illustrandam historiam ecclesiæ Orientalis in terris Coronæ S. Stephani* (2 vols. in 1, Oeniponte: F. Rauch, 1885), pp. 438-442; Plöchl, *Polish Institute,* II (1944), 733.

[60] "In omnibus diœcesibus, ubi essent duo diversi ritus diversæque gentis populi, constans fuit Ecclesiæ disciplina, ut ab unico Episcopo regerentur. Quam disciplinam confirmavit habitum sub Innocentii III Concilium Lateranense, in quo sancitum fuit etiam civitatibus orientali Imperio ademptis, ubi Græci et Latini promiscue commorabantur, latinus Episcopus vicarium sibi subiectum destinaret, qui Græcis iuxta eorum ritum sacramenta administraret." — *Ius Pontificium de Propaganda Fide* (ed. R. de Martinis, pars prima: 7 vols. in 8, Romæ, 1888-1897; pars secunda: Romæ, 1909), IV, 155.

[61] "Nos, matura prius deliberatione habita, dictæ M. Theresiæ Reginæ Apostolicæ

One of the main reasons for the establishment of the Greek diocese was the progressive growth and geographical extension of the Ruthenians in this area.[62] The same policy of establishing Oriental dioceses *pleno iure* was also followed in the erection of the diocese of Križevci (in Yugoslavia) by Pius VI (1775-1799) in his Bull *Charitas illa* of June 22, 1777,[63] and also in his Bull *Indefessum* of June 16, 1777, issued for the erection of the Greek diocese of Oradea Mare, which had previously had only an Oriental bishop-vicar, as mentioned above.[64]

This latter policy became the practice in the subsequent establishments of Oriental dioceses, and thus the ruling of canon 9 of the IV General Council of the Lateran fell entirely into disuse. Upon the first partition of

---

precibus indulgere, ac Ruthenorum græci ritus uniti nationem quantum in Domino licet, specialibus favoribus et gratiis prosequi, ... motu proprio et ex certa scientia, deque apostolicæ potestatis plenitudine, officium Vicariatus Apostolici eiusdem ritus alias in dicto oppido Munkács dicta apostolica auctoritate, ut præfertur, designatum, eadem apostolica auctoritate perpetuo supprimimus et extinguimus, ac prædictum oppidum iuxta canonicas sanctiones civitatis episcopali titulo et honore dicta apostolica auctoritate etiam perpetuo decoramus, ... pro uno Episcopo Munkácsiensi eiusdem græci ritus uniti etiam nuncupando, qui omnibus episcopalibus insigniis et privilegiis eisdem modo et forma, quibus cæteri Episcopi græci ritus uniti perfruuntur et gaudent, cum omnimodo iurisdictione episcopali in Græcos omnes unitos in prescripta civitate Munkácsiensi aliisque locis et terris dictæ diœcesis Agriensis existentes etiam perfruuntur et gaudent, apostolica auctoritate præfata similiter perpetuo erigimus et instituimus. ... Sed iurisdictionem suam ordinariam in clerum dumtaxat et populum Ruthenorum Græci ritus uniti aliosque qui eosdem ritus et unionem sequuntur, et degunt tam in civitate Munkácsiensi ... quam in aliis prædictæ Agriensis diœcesibus partibus, simpliciter exercere valeant, exacte servantes et adimplentes decreta omnia ... hactenus edita vel edenda quoad Græcos qui cum Latinis immixti vivunt, quique huic novæ provisioni non obstent." — *Ius Pontificium de Propaganda Fide*, IV, 177-179; *Fonti*, VIII, 615; *Fonti*, II, 221; Hergenröther, "Die Rechtsverhältnisse der verschiedenen Riten innerhalb der katholischen Kirche," — *AKKR*, VII (1862), 357; Arndt, "Die gegenseitigen Rechtsverhältnisse der Riten in der katholischen Kirche," — *AKKR*, LXXI (1894), 230; Plöchl, *Polish Institute*, II (1944), 735.

[62] Fiedler, "Beiträge zur Geschichte der Union der Ruthenen in Nordungarn," — *SB*, XXXIX (1862), 499-500.

[63] *Ius Pontificium de Propaganda Fide*, IV, 224-227; *Fonti*, VIII, 506; Silbernagel, *Verfassung und gegenwärtiger Bestand sämtlicher Kirchen des Orients*, p. 331.

[64] *Fonti*, VIII, 505; Plöchl, *Polish Institute*, II (1944), 741; cf. *supra* chapter II, article 3.

Poland in 1772 the Ruthenians of Galicia came under the Austrian Monarchy. But they already had a well organized hierarchy. A curious fact may be mentioned here. Then, as now, Lwów was the see for three bishops, a Latin, a Ruthenian, and an Armenian bishop, each one having full jurisdiction over the members of his rite in that territory.

Article 4. Among the Armenians

The return of the Armenians to union with Rome was beset with difficulties and persecutions. At the time of their return (1742) they chose a Patriarch who was confirmed by Rome. However, those Catholic Armenians who lived around Constantinople, and there were many, were subject politically for a long time to the schismatical Patriarch, while ecclesiastically they were under the care of the Latin Vicar Apostolic of Constantinople. This is evident from the exhortation of Pius VII (1800-1823) given to the Vicar Apostolic of Constantinople on July 18, 1818, asking him to care for the Armenians and to alleviate the sufferings inflicted on them by the schismatics.[65]

Pius VIII (1829-1830) eventually succeeded with the help of France and Austria[66] in making the Armenians independent of the schismatical Patriarch, and he erected for them at Constantinople a Metropolitan, Primatial see whose incumbent exercised jurisdiction over all Catholic Armenians previously subject to the Vicar Apostolic of Constantinople.[67] In 1867 the primatial see of Constantinople was united with the Patriarchate of Cilicia.

---

[65] "Quid igitur est quod Armeni Catholici adeo partium studio abripi se sinant, ut multa iam passi sint, et graviora pertimescant? Tuum est, Ven. Frater, omnibus animi viribus in id incumbere, ut pristina apud eos pax, et charitas refloresçat . . . ," — *Bullarium S. C. de Prop. Fide,* IV, 273.

[66] *Bullarium S. C. de Prop. Fide,* V, 49-50.

[67] "Quare pro impenso Nostræ affectionis studio, . . . Sedem Archiepiscopalem et Primatialem in Urbe Constantinopolitana pro Armenis Catholicis ibidem, et in reliquo

Article 5. Among the Malabars

At the time of their union with Rome in 1599 the Malabars were under a Latin metropolitan, and were incorporated in the various suffragan dioceses. On May 20, 1887, Leo XIII (1878-1903) separated the Latins from the Malabars by means of his Letter *Quod iampridem*, instituting for the latter two vicariates apostolic, Kottayam and Trichur, with Latin bishops who were obliged to make use of Malabar vicars-general. Four clerics of the same people and rite were to give counsel to the Latin bishops in all ecclesiastical affairs of their rite.[68]

However, on July 28, 1896, the Holy See established three Oriental Vicars Apostolic for the newly created vicariates of Changanachery and Ernakulam and for the former Latin vicariate of Trichur. The vicariate of Kottayam was suppressed at the time, but erected again in 1911. These four vicariates then formed the ecclesiastical province of Ernakulam in 1923.[69]

Ottomanico Imperio degentibus, qui in præsens subsunt spirituali regimini, ac iurisdictioni Vicarii Nostri Apostolici Patriarchalis Constantinopli tam perpetuo erigimus et instituiumus, ... ut Catholici Armeni . . . , proprii Ritus ea ipsa in Civitate Antistitem habeant qui pleno legitimæ iurisdictionis, et auctoritatis iure eosdem moderetur, pascat, regatque." — *Bullarium S. C. de Prop. Fide*, V, 54-55: decree of erection of the archiepiscopal, primatial see given on July 6, 1830. For the appointment of the Armenian Archbishop there see *Bullarium S. C. de Prop. Fide*, V, 56-58; cf. *Fonti*, II, 233; Silbernagel, *Verfassung und gegenwärtiger Bestand sämtlicher Kirchen des Orients*, p. 344; Hergenröther, "Die Rechtsverhältnisse der verschiedenen Riten innerhalb der katholischen Kirche," — *AKKR*, VII (1862), 361.

[68] "Itaque motu proprio, atque ex certa scientia ac matura deliberatione Nostris, præsertim vi mandamus, ut peracta rituali separatione Catholicorum Syro-Malabarentium a Latinis, duo pro illis constituantur Vicariatus Apostolici committendi Episcopis Latinis, qui sibi assumant Vicarium Generalem Syro-Malabarensem privilegio condecorandum exercendi proprio ritu Pontificalia, et Confirmationis Sacramentum, Chrismate tamen ab Episcopo consecrato conferendi: nec non alios quatuor viros ecclesiasticos eiusdem gentis et ritus eligant, quorum consilio in omnibus ecclesiasticis negotiis utantur." — *Acta Sanctæ Sedis*, XIX (1886-1887), 513 (hereafter cited *ASS*); Silbernagel, *Verfassung und gegenwärtiger Bestand sämtlicher Kirchen des Orients*, p. 358; Arndt, "Die gegenseitigen Rechtsverhältnisse der verschiedenen Riten innerhalb der katholischen Kirche," — *AKKR*, LXXI (1894), 231.

[69] *Statistica*, pp. 251-253.

CHAPTER III

THE CATHOLIC ORIENTALS IN THE UNITED STATES OF AMERICA

Article 1. History and Legislation

Generally it may be said that the people of the various Oriental rites started to emigrate to the United States of America around the year 1880. The Croatians, however, had arrived here somewhat earlier. The year 1880 marks the entrance of the Ruthenians, the most numerous of all of the Orientals in the United States. The Hungarians came in the same year. Other Orientals followed shortly; the Melkites in 1886, the Rumanians in 1900, the Italo-Albanians in 1904, the Bulgarians in 1906. The influx of Croatians reached its highest point in 1907, when 22,828 arrived in the United States. A few Chaldeans, Syrians, and even Copts emigrated to the United States before 1911. Of the Copts no trace can any longer be found at the present.[1]

Though many of the emigrants were of the Greek "Orthodox" religion, Orientals of the Catholic faith were also numerous. It was only natural that instructions from Rome were necessary to guide the bishops of the United States in their dealings with the Orientals, as their arrival presented an entirely new problem in the United States. A fragment of a letter of the Sacred Congregation of the Propagation of the Faith on May 12, 1890, to the Archbishop of Paris on the same problem clarified the position and jurisdiction of the patriarch of the territory from which the Orientals emigrated. It stated clearly the principle emphasized so often in the past, namely, that the

[1] Pallen, *A Memorial of Andrew J. Shipman, His Life and Writings* (New York: Encyclopedia Press, Inc., 1916), pp. 81-239.

patriarch had no jurisdiction over his subjects once they had left the patriarchate, but that the Latin ordinary into whose territory the Orientals had immigrated had full jurisdiction over them.[2]

Following closely upon these emigrants came the priests who wished to take care of their brethren in the United States. The Sacred Congregation for the Propagation of the Faith on October 1, 1890, in an Encyclical Letter provided that these priests were to write to this Congregation, mentioning the diocese which they intended to leave, and indicating the ordinary in whose diocese they wished to work. Again it was stated that they were subject to these ordinaries.[3]

Two years later, on May 10, 1892, another letter of the Sacred Congregation for the Propagation of the Faith, addressed to the Archbishop of Baltimore, provided that only celibate priests were allowed to go to the United States and to receive faculties from their local ordinaries to whom they were subject. Furthermore, all those who were married were to be sent back, since the appearance of the married Oriental priests caused trouble and scandal.[4] Again, with regard to the United States of America the Sacred Congregation for the Propagation of the Faith finally ruled on April 12, 1894, that they needed the written permission of this Congregation, which permission

---

[2] "Maxima est generalis huius sacræ Congregationis quod Patriarchæ ritus orientalis exercere nequeant propriam iurisdictionem extra eorumdem Patriarchatus; et consequenter quod sacerdotes et fideles cuiuslibet ritus orientalis, domicilium habentes extra respectivos patriarchatus, sive etiam intra limitem eorumdem, sed non habentes parochos proprii ritus, subiiciantur ordinario latino loci, in quo morantur, præcipue in Diœcesibus latinis." — *Acta Sanctæ Sedis*, XXIV (1891-1892), 390.

[3] "Huic S. C. debent in scriptis manifestare quænam sit diœcesis ad quam pergere exoptant, ut res deducatur ad notitiam Ordinarii eiusdem diœceseos. Sistere se debent coram Ordinario illius diœcesis in qua sacrum ministerium exercere vellent, ut ab eo facultates opportunas implorent. Memorati Sacerdotes eorumdem Ordinariorum iurisdictioni subesse debent." — *Fontes*, n. 4939, note 3.

[4] *AKKR*, LXVIII (1892), 442; Arndt, "Die gegenseitigen Rechtsverhältnisse der verschiedenen Riten innerhalb der katholischen Kirche," — *AKKR*, LXXI (1894), 236.

they were to show the ordinary to whom they were to be subject.[5]

On November 30, 1894, Leo XIII in his Apostolic Letter *Orientalium dignitas* definitely stressed the principle that Orientals outside of their Patriarchate were subject to the Latin ordinaries in all matters of administration, but that they likewise continued to pertain to their proper rite.[6] This general rule was again emphasized for the Orientals in the United States by the Sacred Congregation for the Propagation of the Faith in a Decree of May 1, 1897.[7]

However, as the Ruthenians increased in number, the Holy See issued the Apostolic Letter *Ea semper* on June 13, 1907, creating a Ruthenian bishop who had no ordinary jurisdiction, but received all his faculties from the various ordinaries in whose dioceses Ruthenians dwelled.[8] This arrangement along with the provisions incidental to the administration of the needs of the Ruthenians proved difficult in its execution. Therefore the Decree *Cum Episcopo* of August 17, 1914, was issued, providing for a bishop with full and ordinary jurisdiction for the faith-

---

[5] *Collectanea S. Congregationis de Propaganda Fide* (2 vols., Romæ: ex Typographia Polyglotta Vaticana, 1907), n. 1866 (hereafter cited *Collectanea*).

[6] N. IX: "Quicumque orientalis, extra patriarchale territorium commorans, sub administratione sit cleri latini, ritui tamen suo permanebit adscriptus; ita ut, nihil diuturnitate aliave causa ulla suffragante, recidat in ditionem Patriarchæ, simul ac in eius territorium revenerit." — *Fontes*, n. 627. Cf. Gulovich, "Matrimonial Laws of the Catholic Eastern Churches," — *The Jurist*, IV (1944), 241.

[7] "Quodcirca orientalium in America Septentrionali degentium potestatem recognovit proprium exercendi ritum, at simul ipsis subiectionem debitam latinis Ordinariis enixe commendavit." — *Collectanea*, n. 1966.

[8] Art. 2: "Episcopus rutheni ritus sub immediate huius Apostolicæ Sedis iurisdictione ac potestate est, ac sub vigilantia Delegati Apostolici Washington[i]ensis. Iurisdictionem autem ordinarium nullam habet, sed tantummodo sibi delegandam a singulis Ordinariis in quorum diœcesi Rutheni commorantur. Eius officium est circa ritus rutheni integritatem vigilare, sacra olea pro Ruthenis conficere, ecclesias rutheni ritus dedicare, Confirmationem Ruthenis ministrare, pontificalia in ecclesiis Ruthenorum peragere, et, præhabitis in singulis casibus litteris dimissoriis Ordinarii loci, clericos rutheni ritus ordinare." — *AKKR*, LXXXVIII (1908), 331.

ful of the Ruthenian rite, and setting forth a series of rules and regulations for the administration of all matters touching the Ruthenians.[9]

This decree remained in force till March 1, 1929, when the Sacred Congregation for the Oriental Church issued a new Decree, known as the *Cum data fuerit,* valid for ten years.[10] This latter Decree was renewed with slight modifications on November 30, 1940, and like its predecessor was to continue in force for a period of ten years.[11]

With regard to the other Orientals the Code of Canon Law echoed the prescription of canon 9 of the IV General Council of the Lateran, when it permitted the institution of a special vicar general for Orientals if the number of Orientals in the diocese made such a provision desirable.[12]

Article 2. Present Situation

As is mentioned in Appendix I, the Ruthenians in the United States have their own ordinaries, and therefore are as such outside the jurisdiction of the Latin ordinaries. According to the division of the Catholic Orientals given in Appendix I, there is appended here a list of the established churches of those Orientals who in the United States of America continue subject to the jurisdiction of the Latin residential ordinaries.

---

[9] Art. 2: "Episcopus Græco-Rutheni ritus eiusque legitimi successores in Statibus Fœderatis Americæ Septentrionalis sub immediata huius Apostolicæ Sedis iurisdictione ac potestate manebunt, plenamque iurisdictionem ordinariam in omnes fideles Græco-Rutheni ritus, permanenter vel ad tempus in Fœderatis Civitatibus Americæ Septentrionali commorantes exercebunt, sub dependentia tamen R.P.D. Delegati Apostolici Washingtonensis pro tempore." — *AAS*, VI (1914), 458.

[10] *AAS*, XXI (1929), 152 ff.; Gulovich, "Matrimonial Laws of the Catholic Eastern Churches," — *The Jurist*, IV (1944), 238.

[11] *AAS*, XXXIII (1941), 27 ff.

[12] Canon 366, § 3: Unus [Vicarius Generalis] tantum constituatur, nisi vel rituum diversitas vel amplitudo diœcesis aliud exigat; . . .

Division of the Orientals in the United States subject to the Latin ordinaries.

I. Antiochene Discipline:
  1. Syrians
  2. Maronites

II. Armenian Discipline:
  Armenians (being the only ones belonging to this discipline)

III. Chaldean Discipline:
  Chaldeans

IV. Byzantine Discipline:
  1. Melkites
  2. Rumanians
  3. Russians
  4. Italo-Albanians

This listing shows that in the United States there are eight different rites belonging to four different disciplines, the Alexandrian discipline alone remaining unrepresented in the United States.

Following is a list of the established churches of the Oriental Catholics in the United States as found throughout the dioceses and archdioceses to the jurisdiction of whose ordinaries they are subject.[18]

Archdiocese of Boston, Massachusetts:

Maronites: Church of Our Lady of the Cedars of Lebanon
457 Shawnut Avenue
Boston, Massachusetts

St. Anthony's Church
256 Elm Street
Lawrence, Massachusetts

St. Theresa's Church
106 N. Montello Street
Brockton, Massachusetts

[18] This list has been compiled from the 1945 *Official Catholic Directory* (New York: Kenedy & Sons). The *Directory* list, however, was carefully cross-checked with Eid's, *A l'Ombre des Cèdres* (privately printed, 1940) and with the private information gained from the present writer's correspondence.

Armenians: Church of the Holy Cross
27 Hillside Road
Watertown, Massachusetts

Melkites:

Church of Our Lady of the Annunciation
178 Harrison Avenue
Boston, Massachusetts

St. Joseph's Church
298 Oak Street
Lawrence, Massachusetts

Archdiocese of Chicago, Illinois:

Chaldeans:

St. Ephrem's Church
1054 Oakdale Avenue
Chicago, Illinois

Melkites:

Church of St. John the Baptist
1249 South Washtenaw Avenue
Chicago, Illinois

Archdiocese of Cincinnati, Ohio:

Maronites: Church of St. Anthony of Padua
429 East Third Street
Cincinnati, Ohio

Archdiocese of Detroit, Michigan:

Maronites:

St. Maron's Church
1555 East Congress Street
Detroit, Michigan

Melkites:

Church of Our Lady of Redemption
2731 McDougall Avenue
Detroit, Michigan

Rumanians: Church of St. John the Baptist
Victor and Orleans Streets
Detroit, Michigan

Archdiocese of Los Angeles, California:

Maronites: Church of Our Lady of Mount Lebanon
1307 Warren Avenue
Los Angeles, California

Melkites:

St. Ann's Church (with mission attached)
812½ North Hoover Street
Los Angeles, California

Russians:

St. Andrew's Church
453 South Cummings Street
Los Angeles, California

Archdiocese of Milwaukee, Wisconsin:

Melkites: St. George's Church
1617 West State Street
Milwaukee, Wisconsin

Archdiocese of New York, New York:

Maronites:
St. Joseph's Church
57 Washington Street
New York City

Melkites:
St. George's Church
103 Washington Street
New York City

Italo-Albanians:
Church of Our Lady of Grace
18 Stanton Street
New York City

Russians:
St. Michael's Chapel
266 Mulberry Street
New York City

Archdiocese of Philadelphia, Pennsylvania:

Maronites:
St. Maron's Church (with various other stations attached)
1005 Ellsworth Street
Philadelphia, Pennsylvania

Church of Our Lady of Lebanon
321 Lehigh Street
Easton, Pennsylvania

Melkites:
Church of Our Lady of Mercy
9 South West Street
Shenandoah, Pennsylvania

Armenians:
St. Mark's Church
142 North Robinson Street
Philadelphia, Pennsylvania

Archdiocese of San Antonio, Texas

Maronites: St. George's Church
426 North Pecos Street
San Antonio, Texas

Archdiocese of St. Louis, Missouri:

Maronites:
St. Raymond's Church
931 La Salle Street
St. Louis, Missouri

Church of St. Anthony the Hermit
1201 St. Ange Street
St. Louis, Missouri[14]

---

[14] This church is not mentioned in the 1945 *Official Catholic Directory*, but it is mentioned by Eid (*A l'Ombre des Cèdres*, p. 201).

Archdiocese of Saint Paul, Minnesota:

Maronites:

Church of the Holy Family
201 East Robie Street
St. Paul, Minnesota

St. Maron's Church
602 University Avenue, N. E.
Minneapolis, Minnesota

Diocese of Albany, New York:

Maronites: St. Ann's Church
190 Fourth Street
Troy, New York

Diocese of Altoona, Pennsylvania:

Rumanians: St. Mary's Church
Scalp Level, Pennsylvania

Diocese of Brooklyn, New York:

Maronites:

Church of Our Lady of Lebanon
295 Hicks Street
Brooklyn, New York

Melkites:

Church of the Virgin Mary
Amity and Clinton Streets
Brooklyn, New York

Diocese of Buffalo, New York:

Maronites: Church of St. John Maron
41 Cedar Street
Buffalo, New York

St. Joseph's Church
331 North Fourth Street
Olean, New York

Church of Our Lady of Lebanon
1120 Niagara Street
Niagara Falls, New York

Diocese of Cleveland, Ohio:

Maronites:

St. Maron's Church
1249 Carnegie Avenue
Cleveland, Ohio

Church of Our Lady of the Cedars of Lebanon
281 Codding Street
Akron, Ohio

Melkites:

Church of St. Elias
1216 Webster Avenue
Cleveland, Ohio

St. Joseph's Church
467 Locust Street
Akron, Ohio

Rumanians: St. Helena's Church (several missions attached)
1367 West 65th Street
Cleveland, Ohio

Diocese of Erie, Pennsylvania:

Rumanians: St. George's Church
713 Budd Street
Sharon, Pennsylvania

Diocese of Fall River, Massachusetts:

Maronites: Church of St. Anthony of the Desert (mission at New Bedford, Massachusetts)
359 Quequechan Street
Fall River, Massachusetts

Diocese of Fort Wayne, Indiana:

Maronites: Church of the Sacred Heart
1001 West Eighth Street
Michigan, Indiana

Rumanians:

Church of St. Nicholas
4310 Olcott Avenue
East Chicago, Indiana

Church of St. Demetrius (mission: St. Mary's Church at Gary, Indiana)
3827 Elm Street
East Chicago, Indiana

Diocese of Hartford, Connecticut:

Maronites:

St. Anthony's Church
34 New Street
Danbury, Connecticut

St. Maron's Church
613 Main Street
Torrington, Connecticut

Chaldeans: A mission at
New Britain, Connecticut

Melkites:

St. Ann's Church
51 William Street
Danbury, Connecticut

St. Ann's Church
7 Connecticut Avenue
New London, Connecticut

Diocese of Manchester, New Hampshire:

Maronites: St. George's Church
Dover, New Hampshire[15]

---

[15] This church is not listed in the 1945 *Official Catholic Directory*, but it is mentioned by Eid (*A l'Ombre des Cèdres*, p. 199).

Diocese of Mobile, Alabama:

Maronites:

Church of St. Elias
Avenue F and 20th Street
Birmingham, Alabama

Melkites:

St. George's Church
1224 Ninth Avenue, S.
Birmingham, Alabama

Diocese of Omaha, Nebraska:

Melkites: Church of the Holy Saviour
1468 South Third Street
Omaha, Nebraska

Diocese of Paterson, New Jersey:

Armenians:

Church of the Sacred Heart
161 Barclay Street
Paterson, New Jersey

Melkites:

St. Ann's Church
240 Marshall Street
Paterson, New Jersey

Diocese of Pittsburgh, Pennsylvania:

Maronites:

St. Ann's Church
33 Fullerton Street
Pittsburgh, Pennsylvania

Church of St. John the Baptist
1210 Howard Way
New Castle, Pennsylvania

St. George's Church
124 Lincoln Street
Uniontown, Pennsylvania

Rumanians:

St. Mary's Church
McKeesport, Pennsylvania

Diocese of Portland, Maine:

Maronites: St. Joseph's Church
1 Appleton Street
Waterville, Maine

Diocese of Providence, Rhode Island:

Maronites:

St. George's Church
85 America Street
Providence, Rhode Island

Melkites:

St. Basil's Church (Mission: St. Elias' Church, Woonsocket, Rhode Island)
445 Broad Street
Central Falls, Rhode Island

Diocese of Pueblo, Colorado:

Syrians: St. Mary's Chapel
429 West First Street
Trinidad, Colorado

Diocese of Richmond, Virginia:

Maronites:

St. Anthony's Church
507 North 33rd Street
Richmond, Virginia

Church of St. Elias
614 Salem Avenue, S. W.
Roanoke, Virginia

Diocese of Rockford, Illinois:

Rumanians: St. Michael's Church
609 North Lincoln Avenue
Aurora, Illinois

Diocese of Savannah-Atlanta, Georgia:

Maronites: St. Joseph's Church
291 Hunter Street, S. E.
Atlanta, Georgia

Diocese of Scranton, Pennsylvania:

Maronites:

St. Ann's Church
1320 Price Street
Scranton, Pennsylvania

St. Anthony's Church
364 Dana Street
Wilkes-Barre, Pennsylvania

St. George's Church
79 Loomis Street
Wilkes-Barre, Pennsylvania

Melkites:

St. Joseph's Church
130 Chestnut Street
Scranton, Pennsylvania

Diocese of Sioux City, Iowa:

Syrians: Mission attached to St. Joseph's Church
Eighth and Iowa Streets
Sioux City, Iowa

Diocese of Springfield, Massachusetts:

Maronites:

St. Anthony's Church
50 Charles Street
Springfield, Massachusetts

Church of Our Lady of Mercy
70 Mulberry Street
Worcester, Massachusetts

Melkites: Church of Our Lady of Perpetual Help
13½ Houghton Street
Worcester, Massachusetts

Diocese of Syracuse, New York:

Maronites:
Church of St. Louis Gonzaga
519 Rutger Street
Utica, New York

Melkites:
St. Basil's Church
527 Lansing Street
Utica, New York

Diocese of Toledo, Ohio:

Melkites: Church of St. Francis de Sales
Cherry and Superior Streets
Toledo, Ohio[16]

Diocese of Trenton, New Jersey:

Rumanians: St. Basil's Church (Mission: St. Mary's Church at Roebling, New Jersey)
238 Adeline Street
Trenton, New Jersey

Diocese of Wheeling, West Virginia:

Maronites: Church of Our Lady of Mount Lebanon (various missions attached)
2216 Eoff Street
Wheeling, West Virginia

Diocese of Youngstown, Ohio:

Maronites: St. Maron's Church
823 Wilson Avenue
Youngstown, Ohio

Rumanians:
St. Mary's Church
73 South Prospect Street
Youngstown, Ohio

St. George's Church (Mission: St. Theodore's Church at Alliance, Ohio)
1837 Seventh Street, N. E.
Canton, Ohio

---

[16] The *Official Catholic Directory* lists this church as Latin, whereas Eid (*A l'Ombre des Cèdres*, p. 204) lists it as Melkite. This difference in the listing seems accounted for through the fact that the basement is used by the Melkites, and the upper part of the church by the Latins.

From this list it is not to be concluded that Catholic Orientals live only in the aforementioned churches of the various dioceses named. Many are dispersed throughout other dioceses, where they do not have established churches. They frequent Latin churches, or possibly also a Ruthenian church when such a church exists in their place of residence.

PART TWO
Canonical Commentary

CHAPTER IV

PRINCIPLE OF JURISDICTION OF THE LATIN ORDINARY OVER HIS ORIENTAL SUBJECTS

ARTICLE 1. THE PRINCIPLE

The historical survey has shown that while staying outside of their patriarchal territory, Orientals are under the jurisdiction of the Latin ordinaries in all things, the identity of their rite remaining fully safeguarded. This fundamental principle was definitely set down in the Apostolic Letter *Orientalium dignitas*, which Leo XIII issued on November 30, 1894.[1] All subsequent legislation insistently refers to it as its basis.[2] The few authors mentioning the subject enunciate the same principle and draw their conclusions from it.[3]

---

[1] N. IX — *Fontes*, n. 627.

[2] So in a private reply given by the Sacred Congregation for the Oriental Church with regard to the Maronites in the United States — Bouscaren, *The Canon Law Digest* (2 vols., Milwaukee, Wis.: The Bruce Publishing Company, Vol. I, 1934; Vol. II, 1943), I, 4; also in a decree of the Sacred Congregation for the Oriental Church on Oriental clerics going to America or Australia to care for the faithful of their rite — *AAS*, XXII (1930), 99-105; Bouscaren, *The Canon Law Digest*, I, 17-24; again in an Instruction of the Sacred Congregation for the Oriental Church on Oriental clerics in countries other than their own patriarchates or countries — *AAS*, XXIV (1932), 344; Bouscaren, *The Canon Law Digest*, I, 39-42; repeated again by the Sacred Congregation for the Oriental Church in an Instruction on the Annual Report to be sent to the Sacred Congregation for the Oriental Church by priests of the Oriental rite having the care of souls outside their patriarchates under the jurisdiction of an ordinary of another rite — *AAS*, XXXI (1939), 169; Bouscaren, *The Canon Law Digest*, II, 5-6.

[3] Duskie, *The Canonical Status of the Orientals in the United States* (The Catholic University of America Canon Law Studies, n. 48, Washington, D. C., The Catholic University of America, 1928), pp. 35, 67; Coussa, *Epitome Prælectionum de Iure Ecclesiastico Orientali* (2 vols., Vol. I: Typis Polyglottis Vaticanis, 1940; Vol. II: Typis Polyglottis Insulæ S. Lazari, 1941), I, n. 40, c (hereafter cited Coussa, *Epitome*); Petrani, *De Relatione Iuridica inter Diversos Ritus in Ecclesia Catholica* (Romæ: Marietti, 1930), p. 46.

It must be clearly understood that this fundamental principle implies two things. First, it places all Orientals living outside their patriarchal territory under the local ordinaries, and secondly, it limits the jurisdiction of the local ordinaries and takes away from their competence that which strictly pertains to each individual rite. For the Orientals are held to the laws of their own particular rite everywhere. But by virtue of their domicile in Latin territory, they are not held to the disciplinary laws of the local Oriental synods, since they are not subject to the jurisdiction governing the places for which these synodal laws are constituted. On the other hand, they are held to the disciplinary laws emanating from the jurisdiction of the local hierarchy, where they have their domicile, as long as these laws are not detrimental to their respective rites.[4]

Further, because of the spread of Orientals throughout Latin territory, the particular law for the member of each rite is presumed to be personal, and in so far unlike the laws of the Code of Canon Law which are territorial.[5] Therefore, as explained, Orientals living in Latin territory follow their own personal particular law; however, they are subject to the Latin ordinaries who exercise their jurisdiction according to the canons of the Code of Canon Law, and who are limited in the exercise of this office, as mentioned in canons 335-337, only in the things which pertain to the individual rite.[6] The extent and the limitation of such jurisdiction will be demonstrated in the succeeding chapters, in which the order of the Code of Canon Law will be followed.

---

[4] Coussa, *Epitome*, I, n. 31.

[5] Canon 8, § 2; Coussa, *Epitome*, I, n. 31.

[6] Coussa, *Epitome*, I, n. 40, c; Duskie, *The Canonical Status of the Orientals in the United States*, p. 67.

Article 2. The Power of the Oriental Patriarch and the Faculties of the Latin Ordinary

It is true that Orientals living outside their patriarchal territory come under the jurisdiction of the Latin ordinary. But the question may be asked, what power does the patriarch retain over these Orientals, and what is the relation of these Orientals to the patriarchate whence they came. For the Orientals in the United States the following Patriarchs would be involved. The Syrian Patriarch of Antioch for the Syrians; the Maronite Patriarch of Antioch for the Maronites; the Patriarch of the Catholic Armenians and the Katholikos of Cilicia for the Armenians; and the Patriarch of Antioch, Alexandria, Jerusalem, and All the East for the Melkites. Orientals living in the United States under the Latin ordinaries depend on their respective patriarchs only in as far as the liturgical prescriptions of their rite are concerned, in the sense that the patriarch is to communicate to these faithful all things pertaining to their rite in order to help them and promote their spiritual welfare. Aside from this the patriarchs have no jurisdiction whatsoever outside of their patriarchal territory.[7]

The reason why the Sacred Congregation for the Propagation of the Faith, and now also the Sacred Congregation for the Oriental Church, acknowledge the power of the patriarchs *quoad ritum tantum* over the faithful living outside the patriarchates is this: The Latin ordinaries for the most part have no perfect knowledge

---

[7] Leo XIII in his Apostolic Letter *Orientalium dignitas* of November 30, 1894, n. IX—*Fontes*, n. 627; *Synodus Sciarfensis Syrorum in Monte Libano celebrata, an. 1888* (Romæ: Typ. polygl. S. C. de Prop. Fide, 1896), p. 215, 9 (hereafter cited *Synodus Sciarfensis Syrorum*); cf. also the fragment of a letter of the Sacred Congregation for the Propagation of the Faith to the Archbishop of Paris on the authority of patriarchs outside their own territory, as produced in *AAS*, XXIV (1891-1892), 330, as quoted in Chapter III, Article 1; Coussa, *Epitome*, I, n. 135.

of the various Oriental rites, and without a proper vigilance these rites might become corrupted. The patriarchs then are obliged to communicate to the priests having the care of souls over these Orientals the decisions and norms pertaining to the respective rites. But it is nowhere determined how this vigilance is to be exercised, and neither can anything be found on the coactive power of the patriarchs over the faithful dwelling outside the patriarchal territory.[8]

In the past the question has arisen whether the extraordinary or delegated faculties of the Latin ordinary (e.g., the quinquennial faculties) could be applied by the Latin ordinary also to his Oriental subjects. Duskie maintained that these faculties of the Latin ordinary as obtained from the various Roman Congregations, except the Sacred Congregation for the Oriental Church, could not be applied by the Latin ordinary to his Oriental subjects, since the Congregations granting the faculties are not competent for Orientals according to canon 257.[9] Gulovich on the contrary, maintained that the quinquennial faculties could be applied by the Latin ordinary to all his subjects, Latins and Orientals, as long as he did not exceed his dele-

---

[8] "Attamen cum Episcopi latini, plerumque perfectam non habeant rituum orientalium cognitionem; ne corrumperentur iidem ritus ob defectum vigilantiæ, eadem S. C. de Prop. Fide, olim, nunc quoque S. C. pro E. Or., Patriarchis potestatem agnoscit in fideles, extra Patriarchatus degentes, *quoad ritum* tantum. Patriarchæ tenentur communicare cum presbyteris illic curam animarum exercentibus, normas et decisiones quæ ritum respiciunt. Modus tamen quo Patriarchæ valeant, *efficaciter* in ritus vigilantiam, illic exercere, nullibi determinatur. Nec de potestate coactiva Patriarcharum, hac in re, quidquam invenitur." — Coussa, *Epitome,* I, n. 135.

[9] Canon 257, § 1. Congregationi pro Ecclesia Orientali præest ipse Romanus Pontifex. Huic Congregationi reservantur omnia cuiusque generis negotia quæ sive ad personas, sive ad disciplinam, sive ad ritus Ecclesiarum orientalium referuntur etiamsi sint mixta, quæ scilicet sive rei sive personarum ratione latinos attingant.

§ 2. Quare pro Ecclesia ritus orientalis hæc Congregatio omnibus facultatibus potitur, quas aliæ Congregationes pro Ecclesiis ritus latini obtinent, incolumi tamen iure Congregationis S. Officii ad normam can. 247. Duskie, *The Canonical Status of the Orientals in the United States,* pp. 69, 178.

gation.[10] A new contribution to the discussion was made by Dr. Plöchl of the Catholic University of America, when he received a private reply from the Sacred Congregation for the Oriental Church through Dr. Herman, a consultor of this Congregation, in answer to an inquiry. To the question, "to what extent can the faculties of the Latin Ordinaries be applied to the Orientals," the following answer was received:

> *"The Oriental Congregation readily extends the faculties of the Latin Ordinaries also to the Orientals, but such an 'extensio' is necessary that the Latin Ordinary can use the faculties for Orientals."*

Dr. Herman added the following remark by way of explanation: "This concerns the extraordinary faculties, e.g., the *quinquennales,* which are granted by the Congregations to the bishops. Concerning the powers to grant dispensations from the matrimonial impediments, etc., as cited in the Code, one must naturally investigate in every single case whether and to what extent the Orientals are included in the canons."[11]

Upon the publication of this information Father Gulovich receded from his previous opinion. He gave as

---

[10] Gulovich, "Matrimonial Laws of the Catholic Eastern Churches," — *The Jurist,* IV (1944), 242-243.

[11] Plöchl, "Quinquennial Faculties extended by the S. Congregation for the Oriental Church to Latin Ordinaries," — *The Jurist,* VI (1946), 75-76. The reply mentioned was dated January 24, 1945. In the original text it reads as follows: "Die dritte Frage, wie weit die Fakultäten der lateinischen Ordinarien auf die Orientalen angewandt werden können, wurde mir so beantwortet:

"Die Orientalische Kongregation dehnt bereitwillig die Fakultäten der lateinischen Ordinarien auch auf die Orientalen aus, aber eine solche 'extensio' ist notwendig, damit der lateinische Ordinarius die Fakultäten den Orientalen gegenüber gebrauchen kann.

"Es handelt sich hier um die ausserordentlichen Fakultäten, z.B. die quinquennales, die von den Kongregationen den Bischöfen verliehen werden. Was die im Codex aufgeführten Vollmachten, Dispensationen von Ehehindernissen usw. angeht, so muss man natürlich im Einzelfall zusehen, ob und inwieweit die Orientalen in den canones einbegriffen sind."

reason that the reply of the Sacred Congregation for the Oriental Church solved and settled this matter.[12] Accordingly the most feasible solution of this problem is for the Latin ordinaries who have Oriental subjects to ask the Sacred Congregation for the Oriental Church to extend the use of these faculties also to their Oriental subjects.

However, even this answer from the Sacred Congregation for the Oriental Church leaves open a question concerning the faculties of the Latin ordinaries given to them by the Holy Office. For as canon 257, § 2 states, the right of the Holy Office remains untouched by the power granted to the Sacred Congregation for the Oriental Church. Therefore, the Latin ordinaries can use validly the faculties received from the Holy Office, which concern especially mixed religion, disparity of cult and the Pauline Privilege, in favor also of the Orientals, since even the Sacred Congregation for the Oriental Church is required to approach the Holy Office for faculties in these cases. Duskie maintains that "proper procedure" in these cases also demands the intervention of the Sacred Congregation for the Oriental Church.[13] However, the omission of the "proper procedure" does not seem to invalidate the dispensations granted by the Latin ordinaries in favor of their Oriental subjects in virtue of the faculties received from the Holy Office.

Similarly the Sacred Penitentiary is also competent for Orientals with regard to things pertaining to the internal forum, even non-sacramental.[14]

Another question deals with the possible assimilation of the faculties of a Latin ordinary with those which are

---

[12] The writer was authorized by Father Gulovich in a letter dated February 25, 1946, to make this statement.

[13] *The Canonical Status of the Orientals in the United States*, p. 179.

[14] Reply of the Sacred Congregation for the Oriental Church, July 26, 1930 — *AAS*, XXII (1930), 349; Bouscaren, *The Canon Law Digest*, I, 174.

possessed by the Oriental bishop. Gulovich maintains that "the Latin bishops may also use the faculties which the Oriental discipline grants to bishops in regard to dispensing from prohibitive impediments, with the exception of mixed religion and the simple vow of chastity."[15]

But it seems questionable whether a Latin ordinary receives the power attributed by the Oriental disciplines to the office of an Oriental bishop, simply in view and through the fact that he has some Oriental subjects. Of course, here are understood only those powers attributed by the various Oriental disciplines to their respective ordinary in virtue of their office and among them only those powers which are peculiar to their rite and which differ from those which the Latin ordinary possesses in virtue of his office. All other powers of the office of an ordinary, whether the ordinary be a Latin or an Oriental, which are the same in the Oriental as well as in the Latin Church, may be used by the Latin ordinary also in favor of his Oriental subjects. If a Latin ordinary feels any deficiency in his faculties for his Oriental subjects, then this deficiency can always be supplied by the Sacred Congregation for the Oriental Church by added faculties, after a proper request for them has been submitted.

---

[15] Gulovich, "Matrimonial Laws of the Catholic Eastern Churches," — *The Jurist*, IV (1944), 243-244.

CHAPTER V

GENERAL NORMS

Generally the Latin ordinary in governing his Oriental subjects will follow the laws of the Code of Canon Law, to which he himself is bound, respecting, when necessary, the particular law of the individual rites. Accordingly it will be shown, first, how far the Code of Canon Law also obliges Orientals; secondly, how the Latin ordinary is further to govern his Oriental subjects in virtue of the fact that these Orientals have been placed under his jurisdiction; thirdly, how far the Latin ordinary is limited in his administration over his Oriental subjects by their particular law and rite. The first proposition will be dealt with in the next article, while the last two propositions will be treated conjointly throughout this work, in which the sequence of the canons in the Code of Canon Law will be followed.

Article 1. Canon 1 and the Laws of the Code of Canon Law

"Licet in Codice iuris canonici Ecclesiæ quoque Orientalis disciplina sæpe referatur, ipse tamen unam respicit Latinam Ecclesiam, neque Orientalem obligat, nisi de iis agatur, quæ ex ipsa rei natura etiam Orientalem afficiunt."

The Code of Canon Law as such affects only the Latin Church and applies to the members of the Oriental Churches only in matters in which Orientals are expressly mentioned and which by their very nature concern them. Following is a list of canons applicable also to Orientals. In the composition of this list the widest interpretation has been used in judging the applicability of the canons to Orientals, because the placing of Orientals under the jurisdiction of the Latin ordinaries favors such an interpretation in this case. The reason why this procedure is justified is that, even though some authors may disagree in the case of certain canons, the Latin ordinary could still employ these canons in governing his Oriental subjects as long as such an application is not detrimental to their rite.[1]

Applicable to Orientals are the following canons taken from the first book of the Code of Canon Law: Canons: 1, 3, 6, 7, 9, 10-21, 22 partly, 23, 25-27, 28 partly, 29-35, 43, 45-51, 52-61 in general, 63, 66-72, 74-78, 80-81, 84-86.

From the second book of the Code of Canon Law: Canons: 87, 90-92, 98-100, § 1, 102-104, 106 with proper restrictions, 107-110, 113-125, 127-129, 133, 138-145, 147-151, 160, 183-185, 196-197, 199-211, 215, 218-247, 257-270, 312, 318, 328-330, 335-336, 339, 366, § 3, 466, 487, 499, § 1, 542, n. 2, 622, § 4.

From the third book of the Code of Canon Law: Canons: 726-727, 730-733, 737-738, 743, 745-752, 754, 756, 761, 770, 779-782, 786-787, 800-802, 804-805, 807-811, 814-820, 823-825, 827, 829, 832-834, 840, 842 partly, 845, 849, 851, 853-858, § 1, 859-861, 863-866, 870-873, § 1 partly, 881, § 1, 882, 884-890, 893-894, 901-907, 911-944, 948, 951-952, 961, 966, § 1, 968, 971, 1002, 1004, 1006, § 5, 1012-1016, 1035, 1038, 1060-1066, 1068-1069, 1070 partly, 1076, § 1, 1081-1087, 1092-1093, 1097,

---

[1] The doctrine of the following authors has been used as a basis for this compilation: Cappello, *Summa Iuris Canonici* (3 vols., Romæ: Apud Aedes Universitatis Gregorianæ, Vol. I, 2. ed., 1932; Vol. II, 2. ed., 1934; Vol. III, 1. ed., 1936), I, n. 62; Dausend, *Das interrituelle Recht im Codex Iuris Canonici* (Görres Gesellschaft: Sektion für Rechts- und Staatswissenschaft, n. LXXIX, Paderborn: Verlag Ferdinand Schöningh, 1939), pp. 32-34; cf. also Michiels, *Normæ Generales Iuris Canonici, Commentarium Libri I Iuris Canonici* (2 vols., Lublin: Universitas Catholica, 1929), I, 42; Van Hove, *De Legibus Ecclesiasticis* (Mechlinæ-Romæ: H. Dessain, 1930), pp. 5-9; Duskie, *The Canonical Status of the Orientals in the United States*, pp. 57-64; Herman, "De Ritu in Iure Canonico," — *Orientalia Christiana*, XXXII (1933), 152-157.

§ 2, 1099, § 1, n. 3, 1100, 1110-1113, 1116-1128, 1129-1132 partly, 1133-1136, 1137 with proper restrictions, 1138-1142, 1144-1147, § 1, 1148-1150, 1154, 1159-1161, 1187 partly, 1188-1189, 1203-1206, 1211-1213, 1219, § 1, 1223, 1239, 1242, 1243, 1249, 1255-1262, 1264, § 1, 1276-1279, 1282, 1283, § 1, 1284, 1286-1287, 1289-1290, 1296, § 1 and § 3, 1307-1308, 1309 partly, 1310-1313, n. 1 and 2, 1314-1329, 1350-1352, 1372-1377, 1381, 1384, 1385, § 1, 1387-1392, 1395, § 1 and § 2, 1396-1405, 1414, § 1, 1431, 1489-1494 with proper restrictions, 1495-1499, 1509, nn. 1-7, 1510, 1513-1515, 1517-1519, 1529, 1544, 1551.

From the fourth book of the Code of Canon Law: Canons: 1552-1558, 1569, 1597-1605, 1960-1962 partly, 1999-2141.

From the fifth book of the Code of Canon Law: Canons: 2195-2219, partly and with proper restrictions, 2223, 2224, 2226-2228, 2233-2236, 2238, 2239, 2241, 2245-2257, 2258, § 1, 2259, 2260-2261 partly, 2262, 2264 partly, 2265 partly, 2267-2269, 2278, 2286-2289, 2313-2316, 2318-2320, 2332, 2335, 2343, § 1, 2365, 2367, 2369, 2371.

Though many may hesitate to apply so many canons to Orientals in general, the difficulty is overcome by the wider standard of judgment implicit in the matter here treated. Even though it may be controverted whether one or the other canon of the Code of Canon Law is applicable to Orientals, it can be applied by the Latin ordinary to his Oriental subjects, since the only standard that limits him is that the application of the canon should contain nothing detrimental or contrary to their respective rites. Moreover it should be added that the applicability of these controverted canons in the relation of the Latin ordinary to his Oriental subjects is not herein made to rest solely on canon 1 of the Code of Canon Law, but rather on the jurisdiction of the Latin ordinary over his Oriental subjects, to whom he may apply these canons.

Further, Orientals living in Latin territory "ex natura rerum" and in analogy with canon 14, § 1, n. 2, are held to the general and particular laws of the territory which concern the safeguarding of the public order and, except in matters liturgical, determine the formalities of actions.[2]

The canons of the Code of Canon Law applicable to Orientals are, in the case of divergent interpretation, to be interpreted according to their own wording and as explained in the Code, and not according to the laws of the respective Oriental rites.[3]

It is generally conceded that the laws of the Latin Church may be used in supplementation of the laws of the Oriental Church, whenever in a particular case no laws for the Oriental Church are in existence. However, then these supplementary laws as taken from the Latin Church are to be considered only as directive, and not as strictly preceptive.[4]

The Oriental law is not gathered together in a Code as is the law of the Latin Church, and this fact at times makes it difficult to ascertain what the law is in a particular case. Then also the many different rites existing in the Oriental Church aggravate the situation. Further, among these rites many have no set, recently promulgated, written law, but rely solely on old sources, usages, and custom.

---

[2] Van Hove, *De Legibus Ecclesiasticis*, pp. 8-9; Coussa, *Epitome*, I, n. 31; Herman, "De Ritu in Iure Canonico," — *Orientalia Christiana*, XXXII (1933), 155; Cicognani, *Commentarium ad librum I Codicis* (Romæ: ex Schola Typographica "Pio X," 1925), p. 13; Jone, *Gesetzbuch des kanonischen Rechtes* (3 vols., Paderborn: Ferdinand Schöningh, 1939-1940), I, 14-15.

[3] Van Hove, *De Legibus Ecclesiasticis*, p. 7.

[4] Wernz-Vidal, *Ius Canonicum, I, Normæ Generales* (Romæ: Apud Aedes Universitatis Gregorianæ, 1938), p. 116; Cappello, *Summa Iuris Canonici*, I, n. 61; Van Hove, *De Legibus Ecclesiasticis*, p. 7; Cicognani, *Commentarium ad librum I Codicis*, p. 14; Michiels, *Normæ Generales*, I, 47; Coussa, *Epitome*, I, n. 84.

Among the Orientals in the United States subject to the Latin ordinaries the following synods or councils are the major sources for the members of these rites.[5]

For the Syrians: "Synodus Sciarfensis Syrorum, habita in Monte Libano a. 1888."

For the Maronites: "Synodus Maronitarum in Monte Libano a. 1736."

For the Armenians: "Acta et Decreta Concilii Nationalis Armenorum" (held in Rome in 1911).

For the Melkites: "Acta et Decreta Synodi Provincialis Melchitarum a. 1872."

For the Rumanians: "Concilium I Provinciale Alba-Juliense et Fogarasiense" (held in 1872).

The Italo-Albanians in the United States follow the Constitution *Etsi pastoralis,* of Benedict XIV, which was issued on May 26, 1742, as mentioned in Chapter II, Article 1, II.

For the United States this leaves only the Chaldeans and the Russians without any laws of a recent synod. The Chaldeans held a synod on June 21, 1853, the acts of which, however, have not been approved by Rome.[6] However, the laws in all the above mentioned synods are far from being complete and perfectly adoptable to present needs, and consequently they reveal deficiencies in various respects. The expected publication of the Oriental Code should end this state of confusion.

The following is a summary of the present and preceding chapters concerning the laws to which Orientals subject to the Latin ordinaries are bound.

1. They are held to the laws of the Code of Canon Law obliging also Orientals according to canon 1.

---

[5] Cf. Cicognani, *Commentarium ad librum I Codicis,* pp. 7-8; Wernz-Vidal, *Normæ Generales,* pp. 113-114.

[6] *Fonti,* Serie II, Fasc. XVII.

2. They are held to the particular laws of their own rite especially in the matters explained below.

3. Orientals subject to Latin ordinaries are bound by the laws of the territory in which they have their domicile.

In the following instances Orientals subject to Latin ordinaries retain the laws of their own rite.

1. In the laws concerning their personal status, such as those governing the obligations and privileges of clerics and religious.

2. In the laws which in their widest interpretation concern their liturgy, such as those relating to the sacrifice of the Mass, the administration of sacraments, the observance of feasts, fasts and abstinence.

3. In the laws which in view of their innate and joint origin are in any way connected with the above mentioned matters, such as any laws concerning the sacraments, matrimonial impediments, irregularities, etc.

In respect to all these laws the Latin ordinaries, follow the repeatedly expressed desire of the Roman Pontiffs, are requested to safeguard the respective rites.[7]

A word may be said here about the Oriental *peregrini* who travel through Latin territory while in the United States. They are naturally not held to all the laws mentioned for those living in Latin territory. However, they are held to the following laws:

1. The laws of their own rite, for the reason that they are personal laws.

2. The laws of the territory where they are actually residing, when the laws concern the safeguarding of the public order and compliance with legal formalities; this conclusion is justified by analogy with canon 14, § 1, n. 2.

---

[7] Herman, "De Ritu in Iure Canonico," — *Orientalia Christiana*, XXXII (1933), 157.

Here an exception is required to be made in favor of the laws of their own rite if a conflict should arise.

3. The laws of the Code of Canon Law which oblige also Orientals according to canon 1.[8]

ARTICLE 2. CUSTOM, TIME, RESCRIPTS, PRIVILEGES, AND DISPENSATIONS

Custom. Because of the nature of the matter the canons of the Code of Canon Law dealing with custom apply for the most part also to Orientals. In the present state of Oriental law custom for them is even more important than it is in the Latin Church, since it is a main source of their law.[9]

It is beyond the scope of this dissertation to treat custom as it exists in Oriental law. A difference between the norms of the Code of Canon Law and the provisions of Oriental law may be noted in that no definitely prescribed time exists among Orientals regarding customs against ecclesiastical laws, or customs outside of the law. Papp-Szilágyi[10] regarded a duration of forty years as the minimum, while Coussa states that in analogy with prescription thirty years would suffice.[11] The Latin ordinary should especially guard against customary usages which run contrary to the divine law; he should eradicate such abuses immediately.[12] As a guiding norm the Latin ordinary could use the Instruction issued for the conducting

---

[8] Herman, "De Ritu in Iure Canonico," — *Orientalia Christiana,* XXXII (1933), 157-158.

[9] Coussa (*Epitome,* I, nn. 78-81) treats *de consuetudine* under the title *de fontibus existendi Iuris.* Regarding the use and importance of custom confer, e.g., *Fonti,* Serie II, Fasc. VIII, nn. 96 and 97.

[10] *Enchiridion Iuris Ecclesiæ Orientalis Catholicæ* (Magno-Varadini: Typis Eugenii Hollósy, 1880), pp. 31-32.

[11] *Epitome,* I, n. 80-c. However, it may be noted that in prescription the time may vary, confer *Fonti,* Serie II, Fasc. V, n. 167.

[12] An example of this kind was found among the Rumanians, cf. *Fonti,* X, n. 429.

of the episcopal visitation of a diocese as given for the Melkites, namely to confirm the good customs and to eradicate the bad ones.[13]

Time. Cappello[14] and Dausend[15] apply the canons of the Code of Canon Law on time also to Orientals. Dausend gives as reason why the canons on time should be applied also to Orientals, that they regulate public order, give certain rules of law or describe certain concepts of law.[16] Aside from the fact that the Latin ordinary is to safeguard the peculiarities in the calendar of the respective Oriental rites subject to him, the subject of time has no direct bearing on the topic of this dissertation.

Rescripts. Orientals subject to the Latin ordinary like the Latins themselves may obtain rescripts from their own Latin ordinary and from the Holy See. With regard to obtaining rescripts from the Holy See, it is proper that they first approach the local ordinary, who will then address all matters in which Orientals are involved to the Sacred Congregation for the Oriental Church, which according to canon 257 is competent for cases involving them. However, with regard to things pertaining to the internal forum, even non-sacramental, the Sacred Penitentiary is competent also for Orientals.[17] For the interpretation and execution of the rescripts the Latin ordinary may follow the norms of the Code of Canon Law, which in this regard can be applied also for his Oriental subjects.

From the previous article it can be seen that canon 44 of the Code of Canon Law does not generally apply to

---

[13] *Fonti,* XV, n. 204.

[14] *Summa Iuris Canonici,* I, n. 62.

[15] *Das interrituelle Recht im Codex Iuris Canonici,* p. 32.

[16] Dausend, *op. cit.,* p. 41: It must be said, however, that Orientals reckon their day from vespers to vespers: cf. *Fonti,* Serie II, Fasc. VIII, n. 181; *Fonti,* Serie II, Fasc. XXVIII, n. 127.

[17] So in a reply of the Sacred Congregation for the Oriental Church of July 26, 1930 — *AAS,* XXII (1930), 349; Bouscaren, *The Canon Law Digest,* I, 174.

Orientals. This canon prohibits a subject to petition another ordinary than his own, if the own ordinary has refused the petition, without that such refusal and the reasons for it are mentioned; through the same canon the vicar general is forbidden under pain of nullity of the act to grant favors which the ordinary has refused, and the ordinary is forbidden to grant favors if the vicar general has refused them and no mention was made of the refusal.[18] It seems, however, that this canon applies to Orientals living in Latin territory, for it protects and defends the authority of the local Latin ordinary,[19] and regulates the proper exercise of his jurisdiction, under which the Orientals have been placed.

Privileges. The question of the quinquennial faculties as mentioned in canon 66 has been treated in the previous chapter. It is the duty of the local Latin ordinary to prevent abuses in the use of privileges[20] and to see to it that the granted privileges conform properly to each particular rite.[21]

Dispensations. While the Latin ordinary cannot generally dispense his Oriental subjects in virtue of his quinquennial faculties as explained in Chapter IV, he can,

---

[18] Canon 44, § 1. Nemo gratiam a proprio Ordinario denegatam ab alio Ordinario petat, nulla facta denegationis mentione; facta autem mentione, Ordinarius gratiam ne concedat, nisi habitis a priore Ordinario denegationis rationibus.

§ 2. Gratia a Vicario Generali denegata et postea, nulla facta huius denegationis mentione, ab Episcopo impetrata, invalida est; gratia autem ab Episcopo denegata nequit valide, etiam facta denegationis mentione a Vicario Generali, non consentiente Episcopo impetrari.

[19] Cf. Cappello, *Summa Iuris Canonici,* I, n. 146, 5°; Michiels, *Normæ Generales,* II, 182.

[20] Canon 78. Qui abutitur potestate sibi ex privilegio permissa, privilegio ipso privari meretur; et Ordinarius Sanctam Sedem monere ne omittat, si quis privilegio ab eadem concesso graviter abutatur.

[21] For example, Orientals cannot enjoy the privilege of saying three Masses either on Christmas or All Souls' day, since it is alien to their rite; Benedictus XIV, ep. *In superiori,* 29 dec. 1755 — *Fontes,* n. 437; S. C. de Prop. Fide pro negotiis ritus orientalis, 22 mart. 1916 — *AAS,* VIII (1916), 104-105. Cf. Wernz-Vidal, *Normæ Generales,* p. 115; Petrani, *De Relatione Iuridica inter Diversos Ritus in Ecclesia Catholica,* p. 81.

however, dispense them in virtue of canon 81, if recourse to the Holy See is difficult, if the danger of grave damage is imminent in any delay, and if the matter looks to a dispensation which the Holy See usually grants.[22] Though canon 82, which refers to the laws from which bishops and other local ordinaries can dispense, does not relate to Orientals in general, yet those Orientals who are subject to Latin ordinaries seem to come under the rule of this canon in so far as they are bound by diocesan laws, or by the laws of provincial or of plenary councils, in accordance with the principle stated in the previous article.[23]

---

[22] Canon 81. A generalibus Ecclesiæ legibus Ordinarii infra Romanum Pontificem dispensare nequeunt, ne in casu quidem peculiari, nisi hæc potestas eisdem fuerit explicite vel implicite concessa, aut nisi difficilis sit recursus ad Sanctam Sedem et simul in mora sit periculum gravis damni et de dispensatione agatur quæ a Sede Apostolica concedi solet.

[23] Canon 82. Episcopi aliique locorum Ordinarii dispensare valent in legibus diœcesanis, et in legibus Concilii provincialis ac plenarii ad normam can. 291, § 2, non vero in legibus quas speciatim tulerit Romanus Pontifex pro illo peculiari territorio, nisi ad normam can. 81.

CHAPTER VI

PERSONS

Article 1. Determination and Transfer of Rite

It is most essential that the Latin ordinary know which are the factors determining the rite of his subjects, when the possibility for transfer from one rite to another exists, and how this transfer is made possible. Since it is beyond the scope of this dissertation to treat this matter in detail, only the rules which regulate the determination and transfer of rite will be given here.

I. RULES CONCERNING BAPTISM AS A FACTOR FOR THE DETERMINATION AND THE TRANSFER OF RITE

1. A person belongs to the rite in which he was baptized or in which he should have been baptized, according to the principle enunciated in canon 98, § 1.[1]

2. Children are to be baptized in the rite of their parents.[2]

3. If the parents are of different rites, one of the Latin and the other of an Oriental rite, then their children are

---

[1] Canon 98, § 1. Inter varios catholicos ritus ad illum quis pertinet, cuius cæremoniis baptizatus fuit, nisi forte baptismus a ritus alieni ministro vel fraude collatus fuit, vel ob gravem necessitatem, cum sacerdos proprii ritus præsto esse non potuit, vel ex dispensatione apostolica, cum facultas data fuit ut quis certo quodam ritu baptizaretur, quin tamen eidem adscriptus maneret. Cf. also for the interpretation of this canon the declaration of the Code Commission of October 16, 1919 — *AAS*, XI (1919), 478; Bouscaren, *The Canon Law Digest*, I, 85; De Clercq, "De ritu et adscriptione ritui apud orientales catholicos," — *Ephemerides Liturgicæ*, VI (1932), 475-476; Dausend, *Das interrituelle Recht im Codex Iuris Canonici*, pp. 82-83; Petrani, *De Relatione Iuridica inter Diversos Ritus in Ecclesia Catholica*, p. 26; Plöchl, "Non-solemn baptism and determination of rite," —*The Jurist*, V (1945), 364.

[2] Canon 756, § 1. Proles in ritu parentum baptizari debet. Cf. also De Clercq, "De ritu et adscriptione ritui apud orientales catholicos," — *Ephemerides Liturgicæ*, VI (1932), 476; Duskie, *The Canonical Status of the Orientals in the United States*, pp.85-86; Gulovich, "Matrimonial Laws of the Catholic Eastern Churches," — *The Jurist*, IV (1944), 203-204.

to be baptized in the rite of the father, except when a particular law states otherwise.[3]

4. A particular law exists for the Italo-Albanians, which permits children to be baptized, if the Italo-Albanian father consents, in the Latin rite of the mother, in virtue of the Constitution *Etsi pastoralis,* issued by Pope Benedict XIV, on May 26, 1742.[4]

5. If one of the parents is a Catholic, then the children are to be baptized in the rite of the Catholic party.[5]

6. If Oriental parents, when both are non-Catholics, should offer their child to be baptized in the Catholic Church, they can choose the rite of their child.[6]

7. Oriental converts may join their corresponding Catholic Oriental rite, or, if they prefer, any other Catholic rite, including the Latin rite.[7]

---

[3] Canon 756, § 2. Si alter parentum pertineat ad ritum latinum, alter ad orientalem, proles ritu patris baptizetur, nisi aliud iure speciali cautum sit. For an explanation of the word *proles* confer Dausend, *Das interrituelle Recht im Codex Iuris Canonici,* pp. 84-86; Plöchl, "Non-solemn baptism and determination of rite," — *The Jurist,* V (1945), 383-387.

[4] § 11, X: Si vero Pater sit Græcus et Mater Latina, liberum erit eidem Patri, ut Proles vel ritu Græco baptizetur, vel etiam ritu Latino, si Uxor Latina prævaluerit, id est si in gratiam Uxoris Latinæ, consenserit Græcus Pater, ut in Latino ritu baptizetur. — *Fontes,* n. 328; Dausend, *Das interrituelle Recht im Codex Iuris Canonici,* p. 87; Petrani, *De Relatione Iuridica inter Diversos Ritus in Ecclesia Catholica,* p. 62; Duskie, *The Canonical Status of the Orientals in the United States,* p. 88; Plöchl, "Non-solemn baptism and determination of rite," — *The Jurist,* V (1945), 368.

[5] Canon 756, § 3. Si unus tantum sit catholicus, proles huius ritu baptizanda est. Cf. *Fonti,* II, 549. However, if the non-Catholic party is a schismatic and under no circumstances wishes the child baptized in the Latin rite, but agrees that the child may be baptized in his corresponding Catholic Oriental rite, then his wish may be fulfilled. — Petrani, *De Relatione Iuridica inter Diversos Ritus in Ecclesia Catholica,* p. 63.

[6] Petrani, *De Relatione Iuridica inter Diversos Ritus in Ecclesia Catholica,* p. 64; Plöchl, "Non-solemn baptism and determination of rite," — *The Jurist,* V (1945), 269-370; Dausend, *Das interrituelle Recht im Codex Iuris Canonici,* pp. 89-90.

[7] Goodwine, *The Reception of Converts* (The Catholic University of America Canon Law Studies, n. 198, Washington, D. C.: The Catholic University of America Press, 1944), p. 175; Coussa, *Epitome,* I, n. 39; Leo XIII, litt. ap., *Orientalium dignitas,* 30 nov. 1894, n. XI — *Fontes,* n. 627; cf. for the same also *Collectanea,* n. 1883, nota 2; *Fonti,* I, 501-503; *Fonti,* II, 585; *Fontes,* n. 4777; Petrani, *De Relatione Iuridica inter Diversos Ritus in Ecclesia Catholica,* pp. 43-45; Gulovich, "Matrimonial Laws of the Catholic Eastern Churches," — *The Jurist,* IV (1944), 208-209.

8. Apostates returning to the Catholic Church do not enjoy the privilege enjoyed by converts, as stated in number 7, but they follow the rite from which they fell away.[8]

9. Illegitimate children follow the rite of their mother. However, if the father admits his paternity then the above mentioned rules may also be applied to illegitimate children.[9]

10. Foundlings should be conditionally baptized in the rite of those who will be responsible for their education, but upon eventual discovery of the rite of the parents the law of canon 98, § 1, will identify the rite to which the foundlings belong.[10]

If husband and wife belong to different rites and the wife prefers to retain her own rite rather than to change to that of her husband, then each of them belongs to the proper pastor of their respective rite for sacramental and other ministrations reserved to pastors.[11]

II. TRANSFER OF RITE

1. To transfer from an Oriental rite to the Latin, or from the Latin to an Oriental rite, the permission of the Holy See is necessary.[12]

---

[8] Coussa, *Epitome,* I, n. 39b; S. C. de Prop. Fide, 7 apr. 1859 — *Fonti,* II, 585-587; *Fontes,* n. 4777, nota.

[9] Petrani, *De Relatione Iuridica inter Diversos Ritus in Ecclesia Catholica,* p. 63; De Clerq, "De ritu et adscriptione ritui apud orientales catholicos," — *Ephemerides Liturgicæ,* VI (1932), 478; Dausend, *Das interrituelle Recht im Codex Iuris Canonici,* p. 88; Plöchl, "Non-solemn baptism and determination of Rite," — *The Jurist,* V (1945), 374-378; Capello, *Summa Iuris Canonici,* I, n. 205.

[10] Dausend, *Das interrituelle Recht im Codex Iuris Canonici,* pp. 88-89; Plöchl, "Non-solemn baptism and determination of rite," — *The Jurist,* V (1945), 378-383.

[11] Duskie, *The Canonical Status of the Orientals in the United States,* p. 82. Duskie bases his conclusion on art. 26 of the decree of the Sacred Congregation for the Propagation of the Faith, Aug. 18, 1914 — *AAS,* VI (1914), 462.

[12] Canon 98, § 3. Nemini licet sine venia Apostolicæ Sedis ad alium ritum transire, aut, post legitimum transitum, ad pristinum reverti. "If anyone on his own accord, or

2. The clergy should not seek to induce Latins to join an Oriental rite, or Orientals to join the Latin rite.[13]

3. To transfer from one Catholic Oriental rite to another which uses the same kind of bread in the sacrifice of the Holy Eucharist, the consent of the Oriental bishop from whom the transfer is made, and the permission of the bishop to whom the transfer is made, is required.

This faculty dates from a decree of the Sacred Congregation for the Propagation of the Faith of November 20, 1838.[14] Duskie holds that this provision was abolished by the Code of Canon Law, and that according to canon 98, § 3, the permission of the Holy See is necessary here also.[15] But De Clerq,[16] Coussa,[17] Petrani,[18] and Dausend[19] rightly maintain that it has retained its force, since it is purely a matter of Oriental law, which, except in cases in which express mention is made of abrogation, the Code of Canon Law does not wish to abrogate.

It seems questionable whether Orientals subject to the Latin ordinary in the United States can use this faculty for transferring from one Oriental rite to another which uses the same kind of bread for the consecration of the

---

by authority inferior to the Holy See has transferred to another rite, the transfer would be invalid." — Duskie, *The Canonical Status of the Orientals in the United States*, p. 78; *Fonti*, I, 511-543; *Fonti*, II, 589-593. Cf. S. C. pro Eccl. Or., decr., 23 nov. 1940 — *AAS*, XXXIII (1941), 28; Bouscaren, *The Canon Law Digest*, II, 50.

[13] Canon 98, § 2. Clerici nullo modo inducere præsumant sive latinos ad orientalem, sive orientales ad latinum ritum assumendum. *Fonti*, I, 509-511; cf. also Petrani, *De Relatione Iuridica inter Diversos Ritus in Ecclesia Catholica*, pp. 36-39.

[14] *Fonti*, I, 501-503; *Fonti*, II, 585; *Fontes*, n. 4777; *Collectanea*, n. 878. Cf. also *Fonti*, I, 499-501.

[15] *The Canonical Status of the Orientals in the United States*, p. 80.

[16] "De ritu et adscriptione ritui apud orientales catholicos," — *Ephemerides Liturgicæ*, VI (1932), 479.

[17] "Hæc facultas abrogata non fuit per § 3 can. 98 C. I. C. quia Codex agit de disciplina latina præcipue (cf. can. 1) et per se; facultas autem de qua agitur est inter Orientales tantum, latinos minime afficit. Nisi id explicite dicat, non censetur Codex velle abrogare Orientale ius." — *Epitome*, I, n. 37, nota 31.

[18] *De Relatione Iuridica inter Diversos Ritus in Ecclesia Catholica*, p. 40.

[19] *Das interrituelle Recht im Codex Iuris Canonici*, p. 152.

Holy Eucharist. This decree was given for the Orient, and it contains nothing concerning the Latin ordinary, and its application by the Latin ordinary would go far beyond its intended extension. The Latin ordinary would need the permission of the Holy See according to canon 98, § 3, to be able to permit this transfer. If he were to grant the permission he would not act the rôle of a Latin bishop but the rôle of an Oriental bishop, but this is beyond his power according to the principle stated in Chapter IV. The possibility of thus effecting a transfer still exists in Oriental law, and was not rendered inapplicable by any change made in the Code of Canon Law; but the Latin ordinary is bound by the Code of Canon Law, and consequently cannot permit such a transfer without the permission of the Holy See.

For the same reason a transfer from the Rumanian rite to the Ruthenian, or vice versa, would be impossible in the United States without the permission of the Holy See, even though it would involve an Oriental bishop on the part of the Ruthenian. But since the Rumanians in the United States are subject to Latin ordinaries, and since the Latin ordinaries cannot permit a transfer without the permission of the Holy See according to the Code of Canon Law, such a transfer from the Rumanian to the Ruthenian rite, or vice versa, would also need the permission of the Holy See.

4. To transfer from one Catholic Oriental rite to another which does not use the same kind of bread in the sacrifice of the Holy Eucharist the permission of the Holy See is necessary under any and all conditions and circumstances.[20]

5. A woman whose rite differs from that of her hus-

[20] S. C. de Prop. Fide, decr., 20 nov. 1838 — *Fonti*, I, 501-503; *Fonti*, II, 585; *Collectanea*, n. 878; *Fontes*, n. 4777.

band may upon entering marriage transfer to the rite of her husband, and after the marriage is ended, may return to her former rite, except when particular law states otherwise.[21]

No change of rite is effected by the reception of the sacraments of the Holy Eucharist, of penance, or of extreme unction, or through attendance at worship in another rite.[22]

The Catholic Oriental traveler in the United States is free to conform to the Latin rite, but must return to his own rite when he returns to his native country. However, those Catholic Orientals who are living in the United States, having established a domicile here, are not permitted to transfer to the Latin rite except with the permission of the Holy See.[23]

If parents change their rite, or also if the father of the family alone transfers, then the children follow their rite, or respectively the rite of their father, if the children have not as yet attained the use of reason. If the children

---

[21] Canon 98, § 4. Integrum est mulieri diversi ritus ad ritum viri, in matrimonio ineundo vel eo durante, transire; matrimonio autem soluto, resumendi proprii ritus libera est potestas, nisi iure particulari aliud cautum sit. Cf. Leo XIII, litt. ap., *Orientalium dignitas,* 30 nov. 1894, n. VIII — *Fontes,* n. 627; *Fonti,* II, 551. For the particular law of the Italo-Albanians concerning this point confer Plöchl, "The change of rite *in matrimonio ineundo vel eo durante,*" — *The Jurist,* VI (1946), 277-279.

[22] Canon 98, § 5. Mos, quamvis diuturnus, sacra Synaxis ritu alieno suscipiendæ non secumfert ritus mutationem. Cf. also Duskie, *The Canonical Status of the Orientals in the United States,* p. 83; Petrani, *De Relatione Iuridica inter Diversos Ritus in Ecclesia Catholica,* p. 42; Gulovich, "Matrimonial Laws of the Catholic Eastern Churches, — *The Jurist,* IV (1944), 212; Beste, *Introductio in Codicem* (2. ed., Collegeville, Minn.: St. John's Abbey Press, 1944), pp. 143-144.

[23] S. C. de Prop. Fide, decr., 1 maii 1897: 1. "Fidelibus orientalibus ad Americ. Septentrionalem confluentibus facultas esto, si libuerit, sese conformandi ritui latino; regrediendum tamen ipsis erit ad ritum proprium simul ac in patriam revenerint.

2. Orientalibus qui verum et stabile domicilium in America Septentr. constituerint non permittatur transitus ad ritum latinum, nisi obtenta in singulis casibus venia Apost. Sedis." — *Fontes,* n. 4935; cf. Duskie, *The Canonical Status of the Orientals in the United States,* p. 39; Petrani, *De Relatione Iuridica inter Diversos Ritus in Ecclesia Catholica,* p. 47.

have attained the use of reason but are still minors, then they may choose to follow the rite of their parents or they may retain their own rite. If the children have reached the age of twenty-one, then they retain their own rite.[24]

Article 2. Clerics in General

As can be seen from the canons obliging Orientals in general, as cited in Article 1 of Chapter V, most of the Canons of the Code of Canon Law on clerics in general are of obligation also for the Oriental clerics, who live under the jurisdiction of a Latin ordinary. Some canons more than others belong to the exercise of the Latin ordinary's jurisdiction over his Oriental clerics. But Oriental clerics enjoy the privilege of the forum, and in case they are sued in a secular court by someone who has not obtained permission from the respective authority, they may make an appearance because of the necessity that impends and because of the intention to avoid greater evil, but they must promptly inform their superior from whom the permission should have been obtained.[25]

Similarly Oriental lay persons suing clerics in a secular court need the permission of the Latin ordinary in whose territory the case is being tried.[26] Most of the canons concerning the obligation of clerics may be used by the Latin

---

[24] Cappello, *Summa Iuris Canonici,* I, n. 205 (this reference is taken from the 4. edition of this volume, printed in 1945).

[25] Canon 120, § 1. Clerici in omnibus causis sive contentiosis sive criminalibus apud iudicem ecclesiasticum conveniri debent, nisi aliter pro locis particularibus legitime provisum fuerit.

§ 3. Si nihilominus ab eo qui nullam præhabuerit veniam, conveniantur, possunt, ratione necessitatis, ad vitanda maiora mala comparere, certiore tamen facto Superiore a quo venia obtenta non fuit. Cf. also *Fonti,* Serie II, Fasc. VII, nn. 1035-1044; *Fonti,* Serie II, Fasc. VIII, n. 183; *Fonti,* XV, n. 101.

[26] Canon 120, § 2. Patres Cardinales ... apud iudicem laicum conveniri nequeunt sine venia Sedis Apostolicæ; ceteri privilegio fori gaudentes, sine venia Ordinarii loci in quo causa peragitur; quam tamen licentiam Ordinarius, præsertim cum actor est laicus, ne deneget sine iusta et gravi causa, tum maxime cum controversiæ inter partes componendæ frustra operam dederit. Cf. *Fonti,* XII, n. 263.

ordinaries also for their Oriental clerics, not only for the reason that they oblige Orientals by their very nature, but also in view of the fact that in many cases their own particular law is the same or at least similar. The Latin ordinary may enforce the canons of the Code of Canon Law on clerics in general, and also the same or similar norms of the Oriental law upon his Oriental clerics in virtue of their subjection to him. In such cases the Latin ordinary would not act as an Oriental bishop, because the coactive power made use of by the Latin ordinary is nothing peculiar to the office of an Oriental bishop. But the Latin ordinary possesses this coactive power in virtue of his own office and may exercise this power for the welfare of his subjects and for the better administration of his diocese. Examples showing the identity or at least a similarity of Oriental law with the laws of the Code of Canon Law are the following: Confession for clerics,[27] association with women,[28] things unbecoming the clerical state,[29] the prohibition to act as commercial agents,[30] the application to clerical study and the consequent degree of proficiency in theological knowledge, which latter may be used along with other determinants as a measure in exploring the clerical candidate's fitness for appointment to an office or a benefice.[31]

---

[27] Canon 125. Curent locorum Ordinarii:

1°. Ut clerici omnes pœnitentiæ sacramento frequenter conscientiæ maculas eluant;

2°. Ut iidem quotodie orationi mentali per aliquod tempus incumbant, sanctissimum Sacramentum visitent, Deiparam Virginem mariano rosario colant, conscientiam discutiant. Cf. *Fonti,* II, 63; *Fonti,* X, nn. 282, 283; *Fonti,* XII, n. 265.

[28] Canon 133, § 1. Caveant clerici ne mulieres, de quibus suspicio esse possit, apud se retineant aut quoquo modo frequentent. *Fonti,* VII, nn. 169-172; *Fonti,* X, nn. 288, 289; *Fonti,* XII, nn. 269, 270; *Fonti,* XV, n. 93; *Fonti,* Serie II, Fasc. VII, n. 301.

[29] Canons 138, 139, 140, and 142; *Fonti,* IV, 55; *Fonti,* X, n. 292; *Fonti,* XII, nn. 252, 256, 257; *Fonti,* Serie II, Fasc. VII, n. 293.

[30] Canons 139, § 3; 142; *Fonti,* IV, 59; *Fonti,* X, n. 290; *Fonti,* XII, n. 255; *Fonti,* XV, n. 97.

[31] Canons 129, 130; *Fonti,* X, n. 281.

Incardination — excardination. Concerning the status of those Oriental clerics who come from the Orient to the United States to care for the faithful of their own rite mention will be made later on when the status of these clerics will be treated. However, Orientals who live under the jurisdiction of the Latin ordinaries in the United States and who aspire to the priesthood and later are rightly ordained in accordance with the rule of canon 955, § 2, seem to follow the laws of incardination and excardination as enacted in the Code of Canon Law.[32] Neither is there any legislation prohibiting clerics of different rites to belong to one and the same diocese. Consequently an aspirant to the priesthood, though he belong to an Oriental rite, whose members are subject to a Latin ordinary, if rightly ordained by his proper Latin bishop with the permission of the Holy See, is incardinated in the Latin bishop's diocese.

Article 3. The Latin Ordinary

All Orientals living in the United States but not having their own bishops are placed under the care and jurisdiction of the Latin ordinaries. The Sacred Congregation for the Oriental Church, competent for all Orientals, asked these ordinaries to apply themselves with all zeal, earnestness, and industry to the care of their Oriental subjects in the matter of providing churches and even schools for them without interfering with their rite. The same Congregation thanked the Latin ordinaries for their great charity, which they had shown toward their Oriental subjects.[33]

---

[32] Canon 955, § 2. Episcopus proprius, iusta causa non impeditus, per se ipse suos subditos ordinet; sed subditum orientalis ritus, sine apostolico indulto, licite ordinare non potest.

[33] S. C. pro Ecc. Or., decr. *Qua sollerti,* 23 dec. 1929 — *AAS,* XXII (1930), 99-105; Bouscaren, *The Canon Law Digest,* I, 18-19.

From the enumeration of the Oriental rites and churches as listed in Chapter III, Article 2, it can be seen that in the United States there are eight different Oriental rites subject to the Latin ordinaries. Churches for these rites are established in eleven archdioceses and twenty-seven dioceses, while in many other dioceses Orientals live among the Latins without their own churches inasmuch as the smallness of their number does not warrant the establishment of the latter.

So the Latin residential bishops are the ordinary and immediate pastors, in the dioceses entrusted to them, not only for their own Latin subjects but also for their Oriental ones.[34] It is their right and duty to govern their dioceses and also their Oriental subjects both in spiritual and temporal affairs with the legislative, judicial, and coercive power which they possess and exercise according to the law of the Code of Canon Law, but they must safeguard always the particular rite of their Oriental subjects.[35]

They will guard ecclesiastical discipline against abuses, especially with reference to the administration of the sacraments and sacramentals, the worship of God and the veneration of saints, indulgences, and the fulfillment of last bequests in favor of pious causes. They will watch over the purity of faith and morals, and see that the people are instructed in Christian doctrine and in their rite.[36]

---

[34] Canon 334, § 1. Episcopi residentiales sunt ordinarii et immediati pastores in diœcesibus sibi commissis. Cf. Coussa, *Epitome*, I, n. 218; *Fonti*, X, n. 539.

[35] Canon 335, § 1. Ius ipsis et officium est gubernandi diœcesim tum in spiritualibus tum in temporalibus cum potestate legislativa, iudiciaria, coactiva ad normam sacrorum canonum exercenda.

§ 2. Leges episcopales statim a promulgatione obligare incipiunt, nisi aliud in ipsis caveatur; modus autem promulgationis ab ipsomet Episcopo determinatur. Cf. Coussa, *Epitome*, I, n. 218; *Fonti*, X, nn. 252-253.

[36] Canon 336, §1. Observantiam legum ecclesiasticarum Episcopi urgeant; nec in iure communi dispensare possunt, nisi ad normam can. 81.

2. Advigilent ne abusus in ecclesiasticam disciplinam irrepant, præsertim circa ad-

In the visitation of their dioceses the Latin ordinaries will treat the Oriental churches like the Latin ones, safeguarding those things that are different by reason of the difference of rite.[37]

There seems to be no canonical ordinance which stands in the way of the nomination of Oriental clerics to the diocesan curia, for example as synodal judges and examiners, parochial consultors, notaries, etc.; in fact, the Code of Canon Law mentions in particular the case of the appointment of a special vicar general in view of the diversity of rites in a diocese.[38]

Mention has already been made of the Latin ordinary's power with regard to dispensations for his Oriental subjects, and also of the fact that he has not the same power over his Oriental subjects that an Oriental bishop has. More will be said about the extent and the limitation of his jurisdiction over his Oriental subjects in the matters treated subsequently.

The Chorepiscopus. This institution as such is still in existence with several Oriental rites. In other rites it may be assimilated to the office of deans, protopriests, archdeacons, and *periodeutes.*[39]

This institution occurs only among the Chaldeans and the Maronites as far as Orientals in the United States are concerned. Among the Chaldeans, aside from the fact

---

ministrationem Sacramentorum et Sacramentalium, cultum Dei et sanctorum, prædicationem verbi Dei, sacras indulgentias, implementum piarum voluntatum; curentque ut puritas fidei ac morum in clero et populo conservetur, ut fidelibus, præsertim pueris ac rudibus, pabulum doctrinæ christianæ præbeatur, ut in scholis puerorum ac iuvenum institutio secundum catholicæ religionis principia tradatur. Cf. Coussa, *Epitome,* I, n. 218.

[37] For visitation of dioceses confer canons 343-346. For an analogy with Oriental law confer *Fonti,* X, n. 555; *Fonti,* XV, nn. 203-204.

[38] Canon 366, § 3. Unus (Vicarius Generalis) tantum constituatur, nisi vel rituum diversitas vel amplitudo diœcesis aliud exigat; . . . Cf. Duskie, *The Canonical Status of the Orientals in the United States,* pp. 70-71.

[39] Cf. Coussa, *Epitome,* I, nn. 247 and 243.

that it is a dignity and not an order, the office gives little power to the chorepiscopi. They have the right to select boys which are destined for the clergy, to inquire about the services held at churches and to make a canonical visitation of monasteries and of churches.[40]

The Synod of Mt. Lebanon (1736) for the Maronites attributed greater power to their chorepiscopi. They have the right to confer minor orders (not subdeaconship), to consecrate baptistries, to dedicate altars and churches. Their dignity, conferred upon them through the imposition of hands by the patriarch, gives them also the right to wear a double cross and miter.[41] In the United States at present there are two Maronite chorepiscopi, one in the Archdiocese of Boston, and the other in the diocese of Richmond.

Article 4. Oriental Clerics Caring for the Faithful of Their Rite in Latin Dioceses

The Apostolic See has at all times been desirous to provide for the eternal salvation of the faithful of the Oriental rites who have left the patriarchal territories and dioceses of the Oriental rite and have established their domicile within Latin territory. For this purpose it has enacted appropriate laws and decrees. In order that the faith of these Catholics be best preserved and that they might be able to use freely their own Oriental rite, it asked that priests of the Oriental rite be chosen from patriarchal or other Oriental territories, who could be sent to minister to the faithful of their own rite. In order to regulate this transfer of Oriental priests, the Sacred Congregation for the Oriental Church issued the decree *Qua sollerti,* on December 23, 1929, for Oriental clerics going to America

---

[40] Coussa, *Epitome,* I, n. 246; *Fonti,* Serie II, Fasc. XVII, 63.

[41] Coussa, *Epitome,* I, n. 247; *Fonti,* XII, nn. 226-227, 466, 1168.

or to Australia in order to care for the faithful of their rite.[42]

This decree became obligatory on April 1, 1930, according to its own provision. However, it may be remarked that this is not the only manner in which priests may be provided for the faithful of the Oriental rites in the United States. As already mentioned in connection with incardination, aspirants to the priesthood may come from the faithful of the Oriental rites living in Latin territory themselves. The ordination of these aspirants and their incardination into the diocese entrusted to the respective Latin ordinary may be the preferable solution for the ordinary in providing suitable priests for his Oriental subjects. If such are not available, however, then the provision of this decree would give him an alternate solution. But at times the Latin ordinary will need to install a Latin priest to care for the faithful of the Oriental rite, since circumstances might make a transfer of Oriental priests to the United States practically impossible, perhaps because suitable or sufficient priests may not be available in the Orient itself. Subsequently a summary of this decree concerning the transfer of Oriental clerics is given.

Petition for an Oriental priest. — The petition may be made by various persons, but it must always and finally come to the Sacred Congregation for the Oriental Church. It may most logically be made by the Latin ordinary who, after an investigation of the necessity of an Oriental priest for the respective rite, will notify the Sacred Congregation for the Oriental Church through the Apostolic Delegate of the need and advantage of such a priest. If the patriarchs or Oriental bishops have been notified of the necessity and advantage of Oriental priests for the faithful

[42] *AAS*, XXII (1930), 99-105; Bouscaren, *The Canon Law Digest*, I, 17-24. In treating of the Oriental clerics the writer has made use of the provisions of this decree liberally, since it is basic for their status and work.

of their respective rites in Latin territory, then they should likewise notify the Sacred Congregation for the Oriental Church through their respective Apostolic Nuncio or Delegate, mentioning the place where the faithful reside and the diocese, at the same time also proposing some suitable priest or priests for their care.

The Sacred Congregation for the Oriental Church itself will then through the Apostolic Delegate notify the Latin ordinary to whom the Orientals are subject, asking the opinion of the Apostolic Delegate and the respective ordinary for advice on the need of a priest or priests and requesting the permission of the latter to send those who are needed. The faithful themselves, seeking spiritual ministrations from a priest of their own rite, may also directly communicate in these matters with the Sacred Congregation for the Oriental Church, though it is more appropriate and expeditious if they apply through the local ordinary.

Qualities of Oriental priests. — The priests considered qualified to minister in the United States to the faithful of Oriental rites may be of either the secular or the religious clergy. However, if they are of the secular clergy they must be celibates. Widowers in general are qualified but in regard to them the Sacred Congregation for the Oriental Church reserves its judgment in every individual case. The Oriental bishop or patriarch who is the superior of the priest in question will further furnish testimonial letters *(celebret)* for the celebration of Mass, which eventually are supplanted by a *celebret* from the Sacred Congregation for the Oriental Church. He will also inform this Sacred Congregation of the past record and character of the priest in question, and if the priest is taken from the body of the regular clergy, then the fact of his selection and the requested information, as noted above, shall be sent to the Sacred Congregation for the Oriental Church also by his Superior.

The Sacred Congregation for the Oriental Church and the permission for the transfer of Oriental priests to the United States. — The Sacred Congregation for the Oriental Church exclusive of the ordinaries and patriarchs in question grants in writing the permission for the transfer of Oriental priests to the United States. The same Congregation sends the rescript usually through the Apostolic Delegate to the Latin ordinaries of the dioceses where the priests are to establish their domicile and to care for the Oriental faithful. The permission for the transfer is sent by the Sacred Congregation for the Oriental Church also to the Oriental priests in question, either through the Apostolic Nuncio or Delegate, or with notice to the latter, through the proper Oriental ordinary or patriarch; and in the case of religious priests, through the Superior with notice to the Apostolic Nuncio or Delegate and to the respective patriarch. Accompanying the permission will be a *celebret* valid only for the purpose of the transfer and for the time required for the journey.

The journey. — The Oriental priest is to proceed to his destined place without delay. Upon arrival he must present himself to the local ordinary offering his testimonial letters from the Sacred Congregation for the Oriental Church, and the discessorial letters from his own bishop or patriarch.

The Oriental priest under the Latin ordinary. — The priest is subject to the jurisdiction of the local Latin ordinary remaining incardinated in his original Oriental diocese. The Latin ordinary is authorized to give the priest permission to celebrate Mass, to administer the sacraments, to perform all sacred functions, and to provide whatever is necessary and helpful for the spiritual care of the Oriental faithful. Hence the Oriental priest is under obedience to the local Latin ordinary concerning the spiritual care of the faithful in the church and place assigned to him, and concerning the exercise of his ministry in the diocese, yet the particular rite of both priest and people is always to be safeguarded.

If the Oriental priest wishes to visit the faithful of his rite living in another diocese in order to exercise his ministry there, he needs the previous permission of the Latin ordinary of the diocese in which he has his domicile and the permission of the Latin ordinary whose diocese he wishes to enter. In case the Oriental priest wishes to change dioceses within the United States, he needs in writing the consent of both, the Latin ordinary from whose diocese he departs and the Latin ordinary who accepts him, without that his incardination in his original Oriental diocese is thereby affected. Further, the Latin ordinary who has accepted him must through the Apostolic Delegate notify the Sacred Congregation for the Oriental Church of this change.

The annual report. — The Oriental priest transferred from the Orient and laboring in the United States among people of his own rite is obliged to draw up annually a report on the religious state of the people entrusted to his charge and his fulfillment of his sacred ministry. This report is to be shown by the Oriental priest to his Latin ordinary, who will add, if necessary, his own annotations, authoritatively approve it, and then send the report to the Sacred Congregation for the Oriental Church. In order that this obligation may be more easily fulfilled, the Sacred Congregation for the Oriental Church on November 16, 1938, issued a new decree on the making of the annual report. The Congregation proposed a questionnaire according to which the report is to be drawn up every year.[43] The year for which the report is required is to be computed from the date of the rescript of transfer. The making of the report is of obligation not only for Oriental priests staying permanently in Oriental churches and caring for the faithful but also for those who are active only temporarily, as long as their stay is beyond that of a year. Latin priests in charge of Oriental churches do not seem to come under this provision as it is issued only for Oriental priests.

In view of a further explicit provision of this decree, any Oriental priest coming into a diocese of a Latin ordinary in the United States, even though he shows letters or documents supposedly coming from the Sacred Congregation for the Oriental Church, will not receive from the Latin ordinary permission to celebrate Mass and to exercise his ministry, unless the Latin ordinary himself has previously received a rescript from the Sacred Congregation for the Oriental Church notifying him of the arrival of this priest.[44]

Those Oriental priests who were already engaged in the ministry in the United States before the decree *Qua sollerti* was issued on December 23, 1929, are also bound by the decree, excepting those matters which treat the transfer of the Oriental priest.

A conclusion may be drawn from the content of the decree and from the principle mentioned in Chapter IV concerning the patriarch's or Oriental bishop's power over the priest while away from his diocese. The Oriental priest in the United States under the jurisdiction of a Latin ordinary remains incardinated in the Oriental dio-

---

[43] *AAS*, XXXI (1939), 169; Bouscaren, *The Canon Law Digest*, II, 5. However, the questionnaire is not to be found in the *AAS*.

[44] Confer also the latest decree on this matter issued by the Sacred Congregation for the Oriental Church July 20, 1937—*AAS*, XXIX (1937), 342; Bouscaren, *The Canon Law Digest*, II, 3.

cese to which he belongs, even though he has been withdrawn from the jurisdiction of his Oriental bishop or patriarch, and has been placed under that of the Latin ordinary.

Nothing is mentioned in the decree concerning the removal of Oriental priests while subject to Latin ordinaries in the United States. It would seem that the Latin ordinary is competent. However, notification of such a removal should be sent to the Sacred Congregation for the Oriental Church.

The administration of the Oriental church and the care of the faithful attached to this church. — The Oriental priest will administer the church and care for his people much in the same manner as the Latin pastors care for their flock. The duties of the Oriental priest as well as his rights are similar to those of the Latin pastor, since in many things the rights and obligations of pastors toward their flock are the same in Latin as well as in Oriental law. Differences, however, exist. For instance, in the United States in all the various Oriental rites whose members are under the jurisdiction of the Latin ordinaries, except that of the Maronites, the Oriental priest confers confirmation immediately after baptism; baptismal water is blessed always at the conferral of baptism; and the Holy Eucharist is not carried publicly to the sick. As for the rest of the functions of pastors, canon 462 may be a guide also for the Oriental priest caring for his flock under the jurisdiction of the Latin ordinary.[45]

---

[45] Canon 462. Functiones parocho reservatæ sunt, nisi aliud iure caveatur:

1°. Baptismum conferre solemniter;

2°. Sanctissimam Eucharistiam ... tamquam Viaticum ad infirmos deferre atque in periculo mortis constitutos extrema unctione roborare, ... ;

4°. Sacras ordinationes ... denuntiare; matrimoniis assistere; nuptialem benedictionem impertiri;

5°. Iusta funebria persolvere ad normam can. 1216.

6°. Domibus ad normam librorum liturgicorum benedicare Sabbato Sancto vel alia die pro locorum consuetudine; cf. Coussa, *Epitome*, I, n. 259; *Fonti*, XII, n. 697.

The obligation of the application of the official Mass for the people is generally the same for the Orientals in virtue of their own laws. Its application in the extension as stated in canon 466 applies only to Rumanians and the Italo-Albanians.[46] The number of times this official Mass is to be applied for the people otherwise varies among the other rites according to the prescriptions or customs of each rite.[47]

For the fees the Oriental priest subject to a Latin ordinary follows strictly the customs or laws of the diocese in which he is serving.[48] Concerning the keeping of the church records they follow the laws of the Code of Canon Law.[49]

The rights and obligations of parochial vicars as enacted in the Code of Canon Law seem to apply, to the extent of their possible adaptation also to Oriental parochial vicars, if such an institution is known to the particular rite, or if the institution of such vicars has become necessary in the United States.[50]

ARTICLE 5. ORIENTAL RELIGIOUS

There are no religious communities of any Oriental rite under the jurisdiction of the Latin ordinaries in the United States. Only a few religious, such as the Basilian Fathers of the Melkite rite, and the Mekhitarists of the Armenian rite, have come to the United States to care for

---

[46] Canon 466, §1. Applicandæ Missæ pro populo obligatione tenetur parochus ad normam can. 339,... Coussa, *Epitome*, I, n. 260; *Fonti*, X, nn. 826-829.

[47] Coussa, *Epitome*, I, n. 260; cf. Cappello, *Tractatus Canonico-Moralis de Sacramentis* (3 vols. in 5, Taurinorum Augustæ: Marietti, 1928-1935, Vol. I, ed. altera, 1928), I, n. 870 (hereafter cited *De Sacramentis*, I).

[48] Canon 463, § 1. Ius est parocho ad præstationes quas ei tribuit vel probata consuetudo vel legitima taxatio ad normam can. 1507, 1. S. C. pro Eccl. Or., decr. *Qua sollerti*, 23 dec. 1929 — *AAS*, XXII (1930), 105; Bouscaren, *The Canon Law Digest*, I, 23; Coussa, *Epitome*, I, n. 263; cf. *Fonti*, X, n. 892.

[49] Canon 470; cf. Coussa, *Epitome*, I, n. 263.

[50] Canons 471-478; cf. Coussa, *Epitome*, I, n. 265.

the faithful of their respective rites. As such they are governed according to the decree *Qua sollerti,* as explained in the previous article. However, like the Oriental priests of the secular clergy, while caring for the faithful of their respective rites, remain incardinated into their respective native diocese or patriarchate, so in like manner the Oriental religious in this country still belong to their respective monastery in the Orient.[51]

With regard to entrance into religion all Orientals are bound by the law of canon 542, 2°, which states that they may not licitly enter the novitiate of a religious institute of the Latin rite without the written permission of the Sacred Congregation for the Oriental Church.[52] The reason for the permission seems to be that the entrance would necessarily entail a change of rite. The provision of this canon applies to all Orientals living in the United States as to their joining a religious institute of the Latin rite, whether they be under the jurisdiction of the Latin ordinaries or under either of the two Oriental ordinaries. The Pontifical Commission for the authentic Interpretation of the Code replied in the affirmative on November 10, 1925, to the question whether Orientals who, without changing their rite, are being prepared to establish religious houses and provinces of the Oriental rite, may licitly be admitted to the noviceship in religious institutes of the Latin rite, without the permission mentioned in canon 542, 2°.[53]

---

[51] To treat the Oriental law for religious in detail is a task that lies outside of the scope of this dissertation. However, the interested reader is referred to Coussa, *Epitome,* II, 1-155, where the subject is treated. It may be stated that the Oriental laws for religious, inasmuch as they are personal laws, are out of the sphere of the jurisdiction of the Latin ordinary.

[52] Canon 542, 2°. Illicite, sed valide admittuntur: Orientales in latinis religionibus sine venia scripto data Sacræ Congregationis pro Ecclesia Orientali.

[53] *AAS,* XVII (1925), 583; Bouscaren, *The Canon Law Digest,* I, 298.

Canon 622, § 4, states that the Latin ordinaries should not permit any Oriental to collect money in his territory without an authentic and recent rescript from the Sacred Congregation for the Oriental Church.[54] Since the promulgation of the Code of Canon Law the Sacred Congregation for the Oriental Church has issued further decrees on this subject for the sake of forestalling possible abuse. The decree of the Sacred Congregation for the Oriental Church as issued on January 7, 1930, concerning Oriental clerics collecting or begging alms outside of Oriental countries and dioceses, emphasizes the provision of canon 622, § 4.[55]

In it the Sacred Congregation for the Oriental Church voiced its intention never to grant the permission for begging of money or the collecting of Mass stipends. If in an extraordinary case the Sacred Congregation for the Oriental Church were to grant the permission, then it will limit the permission to restricted territories and notify the ordinaries of these territories. Even then the consent of the local ordinary is necessary before the collection can be made. Moreover, the ordinary does not have the power to permit such collections within his territory, unless he himself has previously been notified by the Sacred Congregation for the Oriental Church either directly or through the Apostolic Delegate of the fact that the permission has been granted and of the reason for it. In confirming these provisions the last rule was again especially pointed out to the ordinaries by the Sacred Congregation for the Oriental Church on July 20, 1937.[56]

---

[54] Sine authentico et recenti rescripto Sacræ Congregationis pro Ecclesia Orientali, Ordinarii latini nec sinant orientalem ullum cuiusvis ordinis et dignitatis in proprio territorio pecuniam colligere, nec suum subditum in orientales diœceses ad eundem finem mittant.

[55] *AAS*, XXII (1930), 108; Bouscaren, *The Canon Law Digest*, I, 27.

[56] *AAS*, XXIX (1937), 342; Bouscaren, *The Canon Law Digest*, II, 4.

Article 6. The Oriental Laity

Since it is the natural right of the laity to receive from the clergy spiritual benefits and the means necessary for salvation, the faithful of the Oriental rites have a claim upon the clergy for their proper ministration to the needs of the faithful.[57] Though it may not always be possible to have a priest of their own respective rite, especially if the number of the faithful is small, yet if their number has increased, the Latin ordinary should try to procure a priest of their rite according to the rules mentioned in Article 4 of the present Chapter. If this is not possible, he should appoint some competent Latin priest to watch over them and care for their needs.[58]

Canons 684 and 685 are of a general nature. They express the attitude of the Church towards pious associations, and indicate the reason why they are instituted, namely for the promotion of a more perfect Christian life, for the undertaking of works of piety and charity, or for the advancement of public worship.[59] There is nothing in the law to prohibit Orientals from forming into associations for the same purpose. Until the second half of the last century there was little legislation or few documents on this subject in relation to Orientals. Recent Synods for Orientals have recommended these associations, and since their provisions are of such recent origin, their text is not

---

[57] Canon 682. Laici ius habent recipiendi a clero, ad normam ecclesiasticæ disciplinæ, spiritualia bona et potissimum adiumenta ad salutem necessaria. Coussa, *Epitome*, II, n. 172.

[58] S. C. de Prop. Fide, decr., 1 maii 1897—*Fontes*, n. 4935; Petrani, *De Relatione Iuridica inter Diversos Ritus in Ecclesia Catholica*, p. 46.

[59] Canon 684. Fideles laude digni sunt, si sua dent nomina associationibus ab Ecclesia erectis vel saltem commendatis; caveant autem ab associationibus secretis, damnatis, seditiosis, suspectis aut quæ studeant sese a legitima Ecclesiæ vigilantia subducere.

Canon 685. Associationes distinctæ a religionibus vel societatibus de quibus in can. 487-681, ab Ecclesia constitui possunt vel ad perfectiorem vitam christianam inter socios promovendam, vel ad aliqua pietatis aut caritatis opera exercenda, vel denique ad incrementum publici cultus. Cf. Coussa, *Epitome*, II, n. 175.

at all unlike that of the laws enacted in the Code of Canon Law.[60]

However, documents concerning the erection of Latin confraternities in Oriental churches are even more scarce. It seems that such action is possible, and an indication of the manner of its execution may be inferred from the power of the Master General of the Dominican Order. The latter, by virtue of general faculties granted him by the Holy See, can erect confraternities proper to his Order even in churches of the Oriental rite with the previous permission of the respective local Latin ordinary. Concerning the ceremonies of the establishment of these confraternities when entrusted to an Oriental priest, one observes that he is required to use the formula used in the Latin Church translated into the language of his rite. The same rule governs the blessing of rosaries, candles, etc.[61]

In analogy with this it may be said that competent authority may establish confraternities, third orders, and pious unions in Oriental churches under the jurisdiction of the Latin ordinaries, as long as it is done with the permission of the Latin ordinaries under whose jurisdiction and vigilance these Orientals are.[62]

---

[60] Coussa, *Epitome,* II, n. 176; *Fonti,* X, n. 122.

[61] S. C. Indulg., 21 iun. 1893 — *Fontes,* n. 5121; Petrani, *De Relatione Iuridica inter Diversos Ritus in Ecclesia Catholica,* p. 53.

[62] Cf. *Fonti,* X, n. 122; *Fonti,* XV, nn. 836-839; *Fonti,* Serie II, Fasc. VII, nn. 632-635.

CHAPTER VII

THE ADMINISTRATION OF THE SACRAMENTS

The Latin ordinary's jurisdiction over his Oriental subjects is especially limited in the administration of the sacraments, since in this matter the Orientals follow their own laws and rite. In their supervision of and the care for these faithful of the Oriental rite some Latin ordinaries will have the assistance of Oriental priests in established Oriental churches, some will find it necessary to place a Latin priest in charge of Oriental churches, and finally, because of the smallness of the number of these Oriental faithful, and because no Oriental churches are in existence some will have only the solution of permitting these Catholic Orientals to frequent Latin churches and to receive the sacraments as Latins do. In the last two instances circumstances may produce unusual problems in the administration of the sacraments by Latin priests to Orientals.

No difficulty exists in the administration of the Holy Eucharist,[1] the sacrament of penance, and extreme unction, or even baptism in the case of necessity.[2]

While the sacrament of confirmation is usually administered by Oriental priests immediately after baptism, except among the Maronites, it will be the duty of the Latin ordinary to administer this sacrament also to the Oriental faithful subject to him in the case of the Maronites, and to the adults of the other rites subject to him

[1] Canon 866, § 1. Omnibus fidelibus cuiusvis ritus datur facultas ut, pietatis causa, sacramentum Eucharisticum quolibet ritu confectum suscipiant.

§ 2. Suadendum tamen ut suo quisque ritu fideles præcepto communionis paschalis satisfaciant.

§ 3. Sanctum Viaticum moribundis ritu proprio accipiendum est; sed urgente necessitate fas esto quolibet ritu illud accipere.

[2] Petrani, *De Relatione Iuridica inter Diversos Ritus in Ecclesia Catholica*, p. 42.

in the cases in which confirmation is to be administered to them separately from baptism, as will be explained subsequently.

However, difficulties may arise if Catholic Orientals wish to receive the sacraments of baptism, of extreme unction, or of matrimony in a solemn manner from a Latin priest. In what church or in what rite are these sacraments to be administered? The question becomes of practical importance especially concerning the sacrament of matrimony, in which the form varies greatly among the different rites. Canon 733, which states that in the administration and reception of the sacraments everyone is to follow his own rite, does not solve the problem entirely. By virtue of its rule the Latin priest is called on to administer the sacraments according to his own rite regardless of the recipient, but by virtue of the same canon the Oriental faithful are expected to receive the sacraments in their own rite.[3]

The Sacred Congregation for the Propagation of the Faith on December 11, 1838, replied to several doubts proposed regarding this matter. The replies as then given may be used as a guide and a norm for the same problems if found in the United States. In case Latin missionaries (priests) are pastors in Oriental churches they may in the Latin rite administer to the Oriental faithful subject to them the sacraments of baptism, of extreme unction, and of matrimony.[4] Latin missionaries (priests) may also administer in the Latin rite the same sacraments (baptism,

---

[3] Canon 733, § 1. In Sacramentis conficiendis, administrandis ac suscipiendis accurate serventur ritus et cæremoniæ quæ in libris ritualibus ab Ecclesia probatis præcipiuntur.

§ 2. Unusquisque autem ritum suum sequatur, salvo præscripto can. 851, § 2, 866.

[4] S. C. de Prop. Fide, 11 dec. 1838: "Utrum missionarii latini possint administrare Orientalibus Sacramenta Baptismi, Extremæ Unctionis et Matrimonii ritu latino in ecclesiis orientalibus, casu v.g. quo missionarius latinus parochi fungeretur officio in iis ecclesiis? — Affirmative." — *Fonti,* I, 443-445.

extreme unction, and matrimony) to Orientals in Latin churches.[5] However, Latin missionaries (priests) acting as pastors in Oriental churches may not administer the sacraments of baptism, of extreme unction, or of matrimony to Orientals in the respective rites of the faithful.[6] These norms amply safeguard the form required by Oriental law for the validity of a marriage, for the Latin form, which thus would be followed, is the strictest of them all.[7]

Following are a few remarks concerning things or matters intimately connected with or necessary for the administration of certain sacraments.

Simony. — Simony, whether it be contrary to the divine law or simply to ecclesiastical legislation, is forbidden not only in virtue of the Code of Canon Law, but also in virtue of identical or similar laws in the various Oriental rites.[8]

The holy oils and chrism. — Generally considered it seems that Oriental priests who care for their faithful under the jurisdiction of Latin ordinaries in the United States will receive their holy oils from their respective Latin ordinaries. This certainly holds true with reference to the consecrated sacred chrism.[9] However, the Oriental

---

[5] S. C. de Prop. Fide, 11 dec. 1838: "Utrum missionarii iisdem Orientalibus eadem Sacramenta *(Baptismi, Extremæ Unctionis et Matrimonii)* possint administrare ritu latino in ecclesiis latinis? — Affirmative." — *Fonti,* I, 445.

[6] S. C. de Prop. Fide, 11 dec. 1838: "Utrum missionarii possint Orientalibus administrare Sacramenta prædicta *(Baptismi, Extremæ Unctionis et Matrimonii)* ritu orientali servando illius ritum, cui administratur Sacramentum, v.g. græcum cum Græco, in casu quo missionarii latini parochi fungerentur officio in ecclesia Orientalium? — Negative." — *Fonti,* I, 445.

[7] Duskie, *The Canonical Status of the Orientals in the United States,* pp. 168-169.

[8] Canon 727; Dausend, *Das interrituelle Recht im Codex Iuris Canonici,* pp. 41-43; *Fonti,* I, 553; *Fonti,* II, 603; *Fonti,* VII, n. 652 (for the Armenians); *Fonti,* X, n. 1102 (for the Rumanians); *Fonti,* XII, nn. 1412, 1367-1368 (for the Maronites); *Fonti,* XV, nn. 734-737 (for the Melkites); *Fonti,* Serie II, Fasc. VII, 1128-1129 (for the Russians).

[9] Canon 735; *Fonti,* VII, n. 139; *Fonti,* X, n. 404; *Fonti,* XII, n. 230; *Fonti,* Serie II, Fasc. VII, nn. 38 and 39; *Fonti,* Serie II, Fasc. VIII, n. 194; *Fonti,* Serie II, Fasc. IX, nn. 369, 382, 463, 550; Papp-Szilágyi, *Enchiridion Iuris Ecclesiæ Orientalis Catholicæ,* p. 225.

priests bless the holy oils whenever they administer the sacraments of baptism and of extreme unction, or at other times also enjoy the faculty to bless them.[10]

Concerning the fees receivable on the occasion of the administration of the sacraments, the Oriental priests follow the custom or laws of the diocese in which they are caring for the faithful of their respective rites.[11]

ARTICLE 1. THE SACRAMENTS OF BAPTISM AND OF CONFIRMATION

The sacraments of baptism and of confirmation are conferred together in the Oriental rites under the jurisdiction of the Latin ordinaries in the United States, with the exception of that of the Maronites.[12] This method of administering the two sacraments together is permitted only if an Oriental priest administers the sacraments. In case a Latin priest has been appointed to minister to the Oriental faithful, the sacrament of baptism will be administered to Orientals by him in the Latin rite according to the rules of the Code of Canon Law and of the Roman Ritual. In the latter case, such an administration

---

[10] *Fonti,* VII, nn. 558-561; *Fonti,* Serie II, Fasc. XXVII, nn. 1, 24, 200; Papp-Szilágyi, *Enchiridion Iuris Ecclesiæ Orientalis Catholicæ,* p. 223; Duskie, *The Canonical Status of the Orientals in the United States,* pp. 146-147.

[11] S. C. pro Eccl. Or., decr., *Qua sollerti,* 23 dec. 1929 — *AAS,* XXII (1930), 105; Bouscaren, *The Canon Law Digest,* I, 23.

[12] Canon 782, § 5; *Fonti,* VII, nn. 76, 144 (for the Armenians); *Fonti,* X, n. 408 (for the Rumanians); *Fonti,* XV, n. 134 (for the Melkites); *Fonti,* Serie II, Fasc. VII, n. 575 (for the Russians); *Fonti,* Serie II, Fasc. XVII, 52 (for the Chaldeans; this citation is taken from the acts of the Chaldean Synod held in 1853, which, though held with the authorization of the Holy See and attended by its representative, P. Benoit Planchet, S.J., was never approved by the Holy See; the acts of the Synod are published and annotated by Jaques M. Vosté, O.P., in the seventeenth fascicle of the second series of the *Fonti*); *Fonti,* Serie II, Fasc. XXVII, pp. 15-19, and nn. 50-57 (for the Syrians: ancient law); *Synodus Sciarfensis Syrorum,* p. 78 (for the Syrians: new law); Papp-Szilágyi, *Enchiridion Iuris Ecclesiæ Orientalis Catholicæ,* pp. 223-224; Duskie, *The Canonical Status of the Orientals in the United States,* p. 92; Petrani, *De Relatione Iuridica inter Diversos Ritus in Ecclesia Catholica,* p. 66; Dausend, *Das interrituelle Recht im Codex Iuris Canonici,* p. 93; Cappello, *De Sacramentis,* I, n. 846.

will not imply for the recipient of baptism any incorporation in the Latin rite.[13] A Latin pastor would obviously not be permitted to administer the sacrament of confirmation immediately after baptism, as is done in most of the Oriental rites, unless he has received the special faculty to do this.[14]

But the Oriental priest who administers baptism to the children of the Oriental faithful under his care is also, except in the case of the Maronites, the *extraordinary* minister of the sacrament of confirmation in virtue of an express or at least a tacit delegation from the Holy See as reflected through ancient custom, even though among the Oriental rites the bishop remains the *ordinary* minister of confirmation.[15] Further Oriental priests, who have the right to confer the sacrament of confirmation may confirm the infants of a different Oriental rite, if in this other Oriental rite the same faculty is possessed by their priests.[16]

While the Code of Canon Law reserves the baptism of adults to the local ordinary, Orientals are not bound by

---

[13] Canons 98 and 756; cf. Chapter VI, Article 1.

[14] Canon 782.

[15] "Minister ordinarius est Episcopus; in Ecclesia vero græca habetur et minister authorizatus, qui est presbyter et respective parochus." — *Fonti*, X, n. 400 (for the Rumanians); *Fonti*, VII, n. 145 (for the Armenians); *Fonti*, XV, n. 134 (for the Melkites; it is also stated there that in case baptism alone is conferred, e.g., inasmuch as it is necessary to baptize the infant immediately after its birth, then, after an investigation regarding the validity of this baptism, confirmation should be conferred, if possible, by the bishop; if this will not be possible, then the pastor should confirm the child at a time when another child of the parish is brought for baptism); *Synodus Sciarfensis Syrorum*, p. 79. The faculty to confirm was restored to the Italo-Albanian priests in 1917. Cf. Duskie, *The Canonical Status of the Orientals in the United States*, pp. 93-94; Petrani, *De Relatione Iuridica inter Diversos Ritus in Ecclesia Catholica*, p. 65; Dausend, *Das interrituelle Recht im Codex Iuris Canonici*, p. 93; Cappello, *De Sacramentis*, I, n. 846.

[16] S. C. S. Off., 22 apr. 1896 — *Fontes*, n. 1178; Dausend, *Das interrituelle Recht im Codex Iuris Canonici*, p. 97. For an exposition on the validity of the conferral of the sacrament of confirmation by an Oriental priest to a Latin see Duskie, *The Canonical Status of the Orientals in the United States*, pp. 95-97; Coleman, *The Minister of Confirmation* (The Catholic University of America Canon Law Studies, n. 125, Washington, D. C.: The Catholic University of America Press, 1941), pp. 124-130.

this provision, and their own law, generally considered, has no such provision.[17] The Synod of Sharfeh (1888) for the Syrians states, however, that the baptism of adults is reserved to the bishop.[18]

If the sacrament of confirmation is conferred on adults separately from baptism, e.g., inasmuch as baptism had already been validly conferred at an earlier time, then the administration of confirmation is generally reserved to the bishop even among the Orientals.[19]

For the Maronites the administration of the sacrament of confirmation is distinct from baptism,[20] and always reserved to the bishop.[21] It is to be conferred between the age of six and twelve.[22] In its administration the particular law of the Maronites permits the use of two forms, one according to their own ritual, and the other according to that of the Latin Church.[23] In fact, the administration of the sacrament of confirmation in the Maronite rite is much the same regarding the ceremonies involved as in the Latin rite.[24]

---

[17] Canon 744. Adultorum baptismus, ubi commode fieri possit, ad loci Ordinarium deferatur, ut, si voluerit, ab eo vel ab eius delegato sollemnius conferatur. Cf. *Fonti*, XII, n. 112.

[18] *Synodus Sciarfensis Syrorum*, p. 72.

[19] *Fonti*, Serie II, XVII, 52; Cappello, *De Sacramentis*, I, n. 846.

[20] *Fonti*, XII, nn. 374, 112.

[21] "Quia vero, tam in nostra, quam in reliquis Orientalibus Ecclesiis, antiquus mos obtinuerat, ut statim post baptismum etiam sacramentum confirmationis conferretur . . . hac tamen in re servandum præcipimus et mandamus, quod dudum a Reverendissimis Dominis Patriarchis iniunctum est, nosque supra de Baptismo monuimus, ne simplices sacerdotes de cætero præsumant, hoc sacramentum *(confirmationis)* administrare, sed illud Episcopi dumtaxat conferant." — *Fonti*, XII, n. 371; cf. also *ibid*., nn. 112, 373, 374; *Acta et Decreta Sacrorum Conciliorum Recentiorum, Collectio Lacensis* (7 vols., Friburgi Brisgoviæ: B. Herder, 1870-1890), II, 123, b (hereafter cited *Collectio Lacensis*).

[22] *Fonti*, XII, n. 365; *Collectio Lacensis*, II, 126, b.

[23] *Fonti*, XII, n. 369; *Collectio Lacensis*, II, 124, c.

[24] ". . .Nos tamen Sanctæ Romanæ Ecclesiæ ritum hac in parte quantum possumus, sicuti in materia et in ministro huius sacramenti, ita et in unctionis forma sequi volentes, prohibemus in confirmatione ullam aliam unctionem fieri, quam in fronte, dicente Episcopo formam eius sacramenti, quæ in Rituali continetur." — *Fonti*, XII, n. 383; *Collectio Lacensis*, II, 124, c; cf. also canons 790 and 780; *Fonti*, XII, n. 382.

From these observations it can be concluded that the Latin ordinary will administer the sacrament of confirmation to all the Maronites placed under his jurisdiction, while he will administer this sacrament only to the adults of the other Oriental rites under his jurisdiction, whenever it has not been conferred together with their baptism. The chrism used in the administration of the sacrament of confirmation by the Oriental priests is to be blessed also by their Latin ordinaries to whom they are subject. It is true that the blessing of the chrism is reserved to the respective patriarchs and Oriental bishops.[25] But the Oriental priests in the United States will receive their chrism from their respective local Latin ordinaries, not only because it would be difficult for them to obtain the chrism from their respective patriarchs and Oriental bishops, but also because they have been removed temporarily at least from the jurisdiction of their respective patriarchs and Oriental bishops and placed under the jurisdiction of the Latin ordinaries.

As for the remaining matters connected with the administration of the sacraments of baptism and of confirmation the Latin ordinary's jurisdiction is limited to a supervision of the administration by the Oriental priests. For the Oriental priests will administer these sacraments according to the laws and ritual of their own rite. Aside from the norms of their own ritual concerning the liturgy of the administration of these sacraments, a divergency of the Oriental law from the Code of Canon Law exists positively only in several particulars, and negatively in that it is at times not quite so detailed as the Code of Canon Law.

---

[25] *Synodus Sciarfensis Syrorum*, pp. 79-80; Cappello, *De Sacramentis*, I, n. 846; Dausend, *Das interrituelle Recht im Codex Iuris Canonici*, p. 98; Papp-Szilágyi, *Enchiridion Iuris Ecclesiæ Orientalis Catholicæ*, p. 226.

Thus Orientals use natural water blessed at the time of baptism,[26] and for the most part also the declarative form in the administration of the sacrament of baptism.[27] In many rites also baptism is conferred by means of immersion; however, even in those rites infusion may be used in case of necessity and for the baptism of adults.[28]

Their particular laws concerning sponsors are not as detailed as those of the Code of Canon Law, though many insist especially on the prohibition excluding schismatics from this office.[29] Spiritual relationship as an impediment to marriage arises not only from baptism, but also from confirmation,[30] except in the Russian rite.[31]

In other points Oriental law and the laws of the Code of Canon Law coincide, as for instance: the prohibition to confer baptism in private houses,[32] the supplying of the ceremonies in case the baptism was conferred out of necessity,[33] and the annotation of baptism and confirmation in the parish registers.[34]

Article 2. The Sacrament of the Holy Eucharist

In the administration of the sacrament of the Holy Eucharist the Oriental priests under the jurisdiction of the Latin ordinaries in the United States follow their rite and particular laws, while they are always under the super-

---

[26] *Fonti*, X, n. 135; *Fonti*, XII, n. 122; *Fonti*, XV, n. 134.

[27] Cf. Cappello, *De Sacramentis*, I, nn. 839-844.

[28] *Fonti*, XII, n. 125; *Fonti*, Serie II, Fasc. VII, nn. 636-637; *Fonti*, Serie II, Fasc. XXVII, nn. 19, 47.

[29] *Fonti*, II, 27; *Fonti*, VII, n. 66; *Fonti*, X, n. 140; *Fonti*, XV, n. 64; *Fonti*, Serie II, Fasc. VII, nn. 666-669.

[30] *Fonti*, X, n. 315; *Fonti*, XII, nn. 285, 286, 288; *Fonti*, XV, n. 64; *Fonti*, Serie II, Fasc. VII, nn. 800-801.

[31] *Fonti*, Serie II, Fasc. VII, nn. 676, 793.

[32] Canon 776; *Fonti*, XII, n. 121; *Fonti*, XV, n. 62; *Fonti*, Serie II, Fasc. VII, n. 642.

[33] Canons 759, 760; *Fonti*, X, n. 141; *Fonti*, XII, n. 114; *Fonti*, Serie II, Fasc. VII, n. 646.

[34] Canons 777-779, 798-800; *Fonti*, Serie II, Fasc. VII, n. 673; *Fonti*, Serie II, Fasc. XXVII, 52; *Fonti*, Serie II, Fasc. XVII, 52.

vision of their local Latin ordinaries. For the sake of facilitating the frequent reception of Holy Communion, the law leaves the Oriental faithful free to receive the Holy Eucharist in any rite, even with a view simply to satisfying their devotion.[35] However, they should receive their Easter Communion in their own rite.[36] For many of the faithful of the Oriental rites this will be impossible, inasmuch as they are under necessity to receive the sacraments from the hands of Latin priests, since in many places no Oriental priests are available. Their personal status and their affiliation with their rite is not affected by the interritual reception of Holy Communion.

Aside from the supervision which the Latin ordinary exercises over his Oriental subjects, the exercise of his power will normally be called upon only on few occasions. Thus it is the Latin ordinary alone who will give the *celebret* to Oriental priests who have established their domicile in his diocese and work among the faithful of their rite under his jurisdiction. This not only holds for the Oriental priests who belong to his diocese by incardination, but also for those Oriental priests who still retain their incorporation with their native Oriental diocese or patriarchate, but have come to the United States to care for the faithful of their rite and have established a domicile in Latin territory, according to the decree *Qua sollerti,* of the Sacred Congregation for the Oriental Church, issued on December 23, 1929.

Articles 8 and 10 of this decree definitely settle any previous doubts whether the Latin ordinary or the Sacred

[35] Canon 866, § 1. Omnibus fidelibus cuiusvis ritus datur facultas ut, pietatis causa, sacramentum Eucharisticum quolibet ritu confectum suscipiant. *Fonti,* Serie II, Fasc. XVII, 58.

[36] Canon 866, § 2. Suadendum tamen ut suo quisque ritu fideles præcepto communionis paschalis satisfaciant. Cf. Cicognani, *Commentarium ad librum I Codicis,* pp. 14-15; Duskie, *The Canonical Status of the Orientals in the United States, pp.* 122-123.

Congregation for the Oriental Church was competent to grant these Oriental priests the *celebret,* when they state that the *celebret* given to these Oriental priests by the Sacred Congregation for the Oriental Church is valid only for their journey from their native Oriental diocese or patriarchate to the United States, and that upon their arrival the Oriental priests are to present themselves to the local Latin ordinary to whose jurisdiction they are subject, and from whom they will receive permission to say Mass and administer the sacraments.[37] The Sacred Congregation for the Oriental Church issues the *celebret* for all Oriental priests coming to the United States for any purpose other than that of exercising the sacred ministry among the faithful of their rite under the jurisdiction of the Latin ordinaries.[38]

Bination is generally unknown among the various Oriental rites,[39] though the trend seems to be now to permit it, if a lack of priests and the need of the faithful necessitate it. Recent Synods of the Maronites and the Rumanians permit the priests of their rite to binate according to the prudent judgment of the ordinary or patriarch.[40]

Since the members of both of these rites in the United States are under the jurisdiction of the Latin ordinaries it seems that a granted permission in accord with the prudent

---

[37] S. C. pro Eccl. Or., decr. *Qua sollerti,* 23 dec. 1929 — *AAS,* XXII (1930), 103-104; Bouscaren, *The Canon Law Digest,* I, 17-24. On the same problem previous to this decree confer Duskie, *The Canonical Status of the Orientals in the United States,* pp. 101-106.

[38] S. C. pro Eccl. Or., decr., 7 ian. 1930 — *AAS,* XXII (1930), 108; Bouscaren, *The Canon Law Digest,* I, 25-29; S. C. pro Eccl. Or., instr., 26 sept. 1932 — *AAS,* XXIV (1932), 344; Bouscaren, *The Canon Law Digest,* I, 39-42; Duskie, *The Canonical Status of the Orientals in the United States,* pp. 106-110.

[39] Cappello, *De Sacramentis,* i, n. 866; *Synodus Sciarfensis Syrorum,* p. 112.

[40] *Fonti,* X, n. 157; *Fonti,* XII, n. 154.

judgment of these ordinaries, is necessary also for the Oriental priests. This exercise of jurisdiction by the Latin ordinaries over their Oriental priests is not a usurpation of the office of an Oriental bishop, since it is nothing peculiar to the office of an Oriental bishop, but rather it is a provision for the care and need of their faithful, be they Latins or Orientals.

Regarding the Mass stipends, the Oriental priests under the jurisdiction of the Latin ordinaries in the United States abide absolutely by the diocesan regulations and decrees, unless the Latin ordinary in particular sees fit to provide otherwise for them.[41]

The priests of the various rites of the Byzantine Discipline celebrate Mass on the *antimension,* a piece of linen or silk, decorated, containing the relics of saints, and solemnly consecrated by an Oriental bishop.[42] This is a typical case where the Latin ordinary cannot act like an Oriental bishop and consecrate *antimensions,* for this power is peculiar to the office of a bishop of the Byzantine Discipline. In order to provide his Oriental priests with this *antimension,* the Latin ordinary will either have to ask for an indult from the Holy See to consecrate it himself, or he will procure it in desired numbers from an Oriental bishop who has this power. In the United States the Ruthenian bishops possess the power to consecrate *antimensions,* and consequently to procure *antimensions* from these bishops is the best solution for the Latin ordinaries with Oriental priests under their jurisdiction.

As for the remaining matters connected with the administration of the Sacrament of the Holy Eucharist,

---

[41] S. C. pro Eccl. Or., decr. *Qua sollerti,* 23 dec. 1929 — *AAS,* XXII (1930), 105; Bouscaren, *The Canon Law Digest,* I, 23.

[42] *Fonti,* Serie II, Fasc. VII, n. 946; Duskie, *The Canonical Status of the Orientals in the United States,* p. 116; Petrani, *De Relatione Iuridica inter Diversos Ritus in Ecclesia Catholica,* p. 79.

Oriental law has the same or similar laws as the Code of Canon Law in the following instances: the obligation for all priests to say Mass several times a year,[43] the faculty for the application of Mass for the living persons and for the poor souls in purgatory,[44] the preparation for the celebration of Mass,[45] the prohibition to say Mass without a server,[46] and the obligation of Easter Communion.[47]

In several instances interritual relations with proper restrictions are allowed by the Code of Canon Law: the distribution of Holy Communion in case of necessity,[48] the celebration of Mass on the altar of another rite,[49] and the reception of Holy Communion and of Holy Viaticum in case of necessity.[50]

Strict differences between the Latin and the Oriental rites are noted especially in the liturgical field, for example, in the following practices: concelebration;[51] the use of leavened bread as matter for the sacrifice of the Holy Eucharist, except in the rite of the Maronites and of the Armenians;[52] the distribution of Holy Communion under both species, except in the rites of the Maronites, the Armenians, the Malabars, the Copts, and the Ethiopians;[53] the rite and ceremonies of Mass;[54] the language used in the

---

[43] Canon 805; *Fonti,* X, n. 806; *Fonti,* XII, nn. 918, 920; *Fonti,* Serie II, Fasc. VII, n. 680.

[44] Canon 809; *Fonti,* X, n. 820.

[45] Canon 810; *Fonti,* X, nn. 808-809.

[46] Canon 813; *Fonti,* X, n. 807; *Fonti,* XII, n. 929.

[47] Canons 859, 860; *Fonti,* Serie II, Fasc. XVII, 58; *Synodus Sciarfensis Syrorum,* p. 92.

[48] Canon 851, § 2.

[49] Canon 823, § 2.

[50] Canon 866.

[51] Canon 803; *Synodus Sciarfensis Syrorum,* p. 112; Cappello, *De Sacramentis,* I, n. 865.

[52] Canons 816, 817; *Fonti,* X, n. 571; *Fonti,* XII, n. 636; *Synodus Sciarfensis Syrorum,* p. 85; Cappello, *De Sacramentis,* I, n. 853.

[53] Canon 852; Cappello, *De Sacramentis,* I, n. 856.

[54] Canon 818; Cappello, *De Sacramentis,* I, n. 869; *Fonti,* XV, nn. 328-329; *Fonti,* Serie II, Fasc. XVII, 59-60; *Synodus Sciarfensis Syrorum,* pp. 102-111.

celebration of Mass;[55] and the time of the celebration of Mass.[56]

ARTICLE 3. THE SACRAMENT OF PENANCE

Because of the peculiar position of the Oriental priests in the United States many problems concerning their jurisdiction to hear confessions and to absolve from reserved sins and censures arise. The Greek-Ruthenian priests work in two dioceses, each of which in its national character embraces the entire United States; the other Oriental priests are subject to the Latin ordinaries and with certain exceptions are not bound, as the faithful entrusted to their care are not bound, by the censures enacted in the Code of Canon Law. From these two factors alone there may arise a multitude of problems which are difficult and at times in practice almost impossible to settle. This article attempts to provide some norms regarding the decisions to be reached in these cases and to give a solution of some of these problems, always within the scope of the subject of this dissertation.

I. THE JURISDICTION OF THE ORIENTAL CONFESSOR

The Oriental priest caring for the faithful of his rite under the supervision of the Latin ordinary will receive his faculties to hear confessions from his local Latin ordinary. This provision certainly holds for those Oriental priests who come to the United States from their native Oriental diocese or patriarchates to care for the faithful of their rite, since the decree *Qua sollerti,* issued by the

---

[55] Canon 819; Petrani, *De Relatione Iuridica inter Diversos Ritus in Ecclesia Catholica,* p. 81.

[56] Canon 820; aside from the Maronites, who in this regard follow the usages of the Latin rite, Oriental rites vary, most of them celebrating the Mass of the Presanctified during Lent except on Saturdays, Sundays, and some special feasts. Cf. Cappello, *De Sacramentis,* I, n. 868; Petrani, *De Relatione Iuridica inter Diversos Ritus in Ecclesia Catholica,* pp. 81-82; *Fonti,* XII, n. 932; *Fonti,* XV, nn. 334-336.

Sacred Congregation for the Oriental Church on December 23, 1929, states this explicitly in regard to these Oriental priests.[57]

Those Oriental priests who belong to a Latin diocese in virtue of their incardination receive the same faculties from their own Latin ordinary after they have been found competent through an examination according to canon 877 of the Code of Canon Law.[58]

The Latin ordinary may attach certain limitations to the faculties of hearing confessions when he grants faculties to his Oriental priests, just as he may in those granted to his Latin priests.[59] However, after the Oriental priests caring for the faithful of their rite have received confessional faculties from their proper Latin ordinary, the Code of Canon Law permits them and any approved confessor to absolve all the faithful irrespective of rite, and likewise grants to all the faithful the permission to confess their sins to any approved confessor they prefer no matter of what rite.[60]

The Italo-Albanian priests are an exception to this rule. In the use of their confessional faculties they are

---

[57] *AAS*, XXII (1930), 104; Bouscaren, *The Canon Law Digest*, I, 22; cf. Duskie, *The Canonical Status of the Orientals in the United States*, p. 139.

[58] Canon 877, § 1. Tum locorum Ordinarii iurisdictionem, tum Superiores religiosi iurisdictionem aut licentiam audiendarum confessionum ne concedant, nisi iis qui idonei per examen reperti fuerint, nisi agatur de sacerdote cuius theologicam doctrinam aliunde compertam habeant.

§ 2. Si post concessam iurisdictionem aut licentiam prudenter dubitent num probatus a se antea sacerdos pergat adhuc idoneus esse, eum ad novum doctrinæ periculum adigant, etsi agatur de parocho aut canonico pœnitentiario.

[59] Canon 878; Duskie, *The Canonical Status of the Orientals in the United States*, p. 126.

[60] Canon 881, § 1. Omnes utriusque cleri sacerdotes ad audiendas confessiones approbati in aliquo loco, sive ordinaria sive delegata iurisdictione instructi, possunt etiam vagos ac peregrinos ex alia diœcesi vel parœcia ad sese accedentes, itemque catholicos cuiusque ritus orientalis, valide et licite absolvere.

Canon 905. Cuivis fideli integrum est confessario legitime approbato etiam alius ritus, cui maluerit, peccata sua confiteri. Cf. Duskie, *The Canonical Status of the Orientals in the United States*, p. 126.

restricted to the faithful of their rite, and may absolve Latins only in the case of necessity. Yet even to the Italo-Albanian priests the Latin ordinary according to his prudent judgment may grant the faculty to absolve Latins outside of a case of necessity.[61]

Because of the freedom allowed by canon 881 for interritual relations in the matter of confessions, the Latin ordinary could appoint, if he sees fit, an Oriental priest as the ordinary or extraordinary confessor for Latin women religious according to the regulations of the Code of Canon Law.[62] Oriental confessors like the Latin ones, unless their delegated powers are limited, may validly and licitly absolve women religious, when, for the sake of peace of conscience they are approached by these religious. Oriental confessors do not possess this faculty in virtue of canon 522 of the Code of Canon Law, for this canon does not affect Orientals; they possess it in virtue of the faculty granted by the Sacred Congregation for Religious for all confessors of the world, which faculty was never revoked.[63]

The Latin ordinary may, for a grave reason, with reference to the Oriental priests who are subject to him as well as the Latin priests, revoke the faculty of hearing confessions.[64]

II. THE ORIENTAL CONFESSOR

In virtue of canons 881 and 905, after having been approved by the Latin ordinary, the Oriental priests can

[61] Clemens VIII, instr. *Sanctissimus,* 31 aug. 1595, § 3 — *Fontes,* n. 179; Benedictus XIV, const. *Etsi pastoralis,* 26 maii 1742, § 5, nn. 5, 6 — *Fontes,* n. 328; Petrani, *De Relatione Iuridica inter Diversos Ritus in Ecclesia Catholica,* p. 87.

[62] In Oriental law similar norms as in the Code of Canon Law exist with regard to the hearing of confessions of women religious of the various Oriental rites. Cf. *Fonti,* XII, n. 345; Coussa, *Epitome,* II, nn. 38-51; Petrani, *De Relatione Iuridica inter Diversos Ritus in Ecclesia Catholica,* p. 89.

[63] S. C. de Religiosis, decr., 5 aug. 1913 — *Fontes,* n. 4418; S. C. de Religiosis, *Romana et aliarum,* 3 maii 1914 — *Fontes,* n. 4421; cf. Petrani, *De Relatione Iuridica inter Diversos Ritus in Ecclesia Catholica,* p. 89.

[64] Canon 880.

absolve any penitent, no matter of what rite. Consequently, if his faculties do not restrict him to his particular Oriental church, but are given for the entire diocese, as they usually are, he can hear confessions validly and licitly upon invitation in Latin churches, or in churches of Oriental rites different from his own, which are subject to the ordinary of the respective diocese. However, the Oriental confessor under the jurisdiction of the Latin ordinary in the United States could not hear confessions in a Ruthenian church, unless he had also received faculties from the Ruthenian ordinary, for he would then, from the juridical point of view as the ultimate determining factor, be in another diocese, even though territorially the Ruthenian church stands in the diocese of a Latin bishop.

Orientals like Latins make use of a confessional located in an open and conspicuous place in the church, and provided with a grating which separates the confessor and the penitent. Oriental law as well as the Code of Canon Law states that confessions are not to be heard in private houses, except the confessions of the sick, or when a case of necessity demands it; this ruling holds especially for women penitents.[65]

Oriental confessors use the language and formula specified for the giving of absolution in confession according to the prescriptions of their own rite.[66] The seal of confession by its very nature obliges Oriental confessors as strictly as it does the Latins.[67]

---

[65] Canons 908-910; *Fonti*, I, 103-105; *Fonti*, II, 165; *Fonti*, X, n. 395; *Fonti*, XII, n. 362; *Fonti*, XV, nn. 125, 126; *Synodus Sciarfensis Syrorum*, pp. 118-119; cf. Cappello, *Tractatus Canonico-Moralis de Sacramentis* (Vol. II, Pars I, ed. altera, 1929) Vol. II, Pars I, n. 1041 (hereafter cited *De Sacramentis*, Vol. II, Pars I).

[66] *Synodus Sciarfensis Syrorum*, p. 117; Petrani, *De Relatione Iuridica inter Diversos Ritus in Ecclesia Catholica*, pp. 89-90; Papp-Szilágyi, *Enchiridion Iuris Ecclesiæ Orientalis Catholicæ*, p. 235; Cappello, *De Sacramentis*, Vol. II, Pars I, n. 1035.

[67] Canons 889-890; *Fonti*, VII, nn. 694-696; *Fonti*, XII, n. 1411; *Fonti*, Serie II, Fasc. VII, nn. 769-710; Cappello, *De Sacramentis*, Vol. II, Pars I, n. 1034; Papp-Szilágyi, *op. cit.*, p. 236.

III. THE RESERVATION OF SINS

The Latin ordinaries have the power to reserve some cases to their own tribunal.[68] Orientals in the United States, except the Ruthenians, have been placed under the jurisdiction of the Latin ordinaries, and are subject to the particular laws of the diocese as long as these laws are not contrary or detrimental to the Oriental rites.[69] Consequently episcopal reservations in force throughout the diocese affect also those Orientals who are subject to the local Latin ordinary.[70] This principle was also stated by Pope Leo XIII in his Constitution *Orientalium dignitas* of November 30, 1894.[71]

Since Oriental confessors, who are subject to the local Latin ordinaries are bound by the episcopal reservations of cases, they seem also to profit by the provision of canon 900, which states the cessation of reservations, a canon as such not applicable to Orientals in general.[72]

However, the provision of paragraph 3 of canon 900, which states that an episcopal reservation ceases if the penitent goes to confession outside the diocese where the case is reserved, does not hold, if a Latin would go to a Ruthenian church, or a Ruthenian to a Latin church, for confession. A regulation concerning this matter in the

---

[68] Canons 893, 897.

[69] Cf. Chapter V, Article 1.

[70] Duskie, *The Canonical Status of the Oriental in the United States*, p. 138.

[71] N. VI — *Fontes*, n. 627.

[72] Canon 900. Quævis reservatio omni vi caret:

1°. Cum confessionem peragunt sive ægroti qui domo egredi non valent, sive sponsi matrimonii ineundi causa;

2°. Quoties vel legitimus Superior petitam pro aliquo determinato casu absolvendi facultatem denegaverit, vel, prudenti confessarii iudicio, absolvendi facultas a legitimo Superiore peti nequeat sine gravi pœnitentis incommodo aut sine periculo violationis sigilli sacramentalis;

3°. Extra territorium reservantis, etiamsi dumtaxat ad absolutionem obtinendam pœnitens ex eo discesserit. Cf. Cappello, *De Sacramentis*, Vol. II, Pars I, n. 1045.

particular law for the Ruthenians in the United States expressly forbids this:

> Priests of the Latin rite, however, cannot absolve the faithful of the Greek-Ruthenian rite from censures and reserved cases established by the Greek-Ruthenian Ordinary, without the latter's permission. The same thing, in turn, is true of the Greek-Ruthenian priests regarding the censures and reservations established by the Ordinary of the Latin rite. And in order to avoid difficulties, which rather frequently occur in practice, let the respective Bishops, if they have any reserved cases, inform each other of the reservations they have made.[73]

The sin reserved to the Holy See, namely, the false charge whereby an innocent confessor is accused before an ecclesiastical tribunal of the crime of sollicitation in connection with the sacrament of penance,[74] and also the obligation to denounce to the local ordinary or to the Sacred Congregation of the Holy Office within one month a priest who is guilty of the crime of sollicitation in confession, bind also Orientals.[75] Oriental confessors are also affected by the prohibition, enacted in canon 884, which forbids the absolution of an accomplice in a sin of impurity.[76]

---

[73] Article 31 of the decree *Cum data fuerit*, issued by the Sacred Congregation for the Oriental Church on March 1, 1929, as reproduced in English by Bouscaren (*The Canon Law Digest*, I, 14); cf. *AAS*, XXI (1929), 158.

[74] Canon 894.

[75] Canon 904; Benedictus XIV, const. *Sacramentum pœnitentiæ*, 1 iun. 1741 — Documentum V in Codice; cf. Cappello, *De Sacramentis*, Vol. II, Pars I, n. 1033.

[76] Canon 884. Absolutio complicis in peccato turpi invalida est, præterquam in mortis periculo; et etiam in periculo mortis, extra casum necessitatis, est ex parte confessarii illicita ad normam constitutionum apostolicarum et nominatim constitutionis Benedicti XIV *Sacramentum Pœnitentiæ*, 1 iun. 1741. Cf. Duskie, *The Canonical Status of the Orientals in the United States*, p. 134.

IV. THE GREEK-RUTHENIAN CONFESSOR

The Greek-Ruthenians in the United States are divided into two ordinariates with their own bishops who exercise complete and ordinary jurisdiction extending to the faithful of their rite throughout the entire United States. Because of this position, they are living territorially in Latin dioceses. The Sacred Congregation for the Oriental Church on August 26, 1932, established the following rule concerning the jurisdiction of the Greek-Ruthenian confessor in his own national diocese, and in the territorial diocese of the Latin bishops.

> A priest of the Greek-Byzantine rite, approved by his Ordinary for confessions, cannot validly and licitly absolve in a church or oratory which is subject to the exclusive jurisdiction of the Ordinary of the Latin rite, unless the latter has expressly granted him faculties.[77]

The Sacred Congregation for the Propagation of the Faith on December 2, 1932, gave the following rule for the Latin confessors and their jurisdiction with regard to the Greek-Ruthenian dioceses.

> A priest of the Latin rite cannot validly and licitly hear confessions and give absolution in a church or oratory which is subject to the exclusive jurisdiction of the Ordinary of the Greek-Byzantine rite, unless the latter has expressly granted him the faculty to do so.[78]

However, the people of the Latin as well as of the Oriental rites are permitted in virtue of canons 881 and

---

[77] Bouscaren, *The Canon Law Digest*, II, 218. This and the subsequent citation were taken by Bouscaren from the *Sylloge præcipuorum documentorum recentium Summorum Pontificum et S. Congregationis de Propaganda Fide necnon aliarum Ss. Congregationum Romanarum*, published by the Sacred Congregation for the Propagation of the Faith in Rome in 1939. The writer regrets that this work was not available to him.

[78] Bouscaren, *The Canon Law Digest*, II, 218.

905, as previously explained, to go to confession to any approved confessor no matter of what rite or diocese.

Article 4. The Sacrament of Holy Orders

The Latin ordinary in caring for the Oriental faithful subject to him can receive competent Oriental priests from two sources. The transfer of Oriental priests from their native Oriental dioceses or patriarchates to the United States as a source of Oriental priests for the Latin ordinary has already been described.[79] Another source is the vocations to the priesthood on the part of the Orientals subject to his jurisdiction. The present article treats the ordination of these Oriental candidates.

I. The Minister of Ordination

Since the Oriental faithful in the United States, except the Ruthenians, are subject to the Latin ordinaries, their proper bishop for ordination is the local Latin ordinary who, however, can ordain them only upon having obtained an Apostolic indult.[80]

Although Pope Celestine III (1191-1198) forbade any interchange of rite in the reception of sacred orders,[81] Pope Innocent III (1198-1216) stated that Orientals subject to Latin ordinaries should be ordained by the latter.[82]

Pope Benedict XIV in his Constitution *Etsi pastoralis*,

---

[79] Chapter VI, Article 4.

[80] Canon 955, § 2. Episcopus proprius, iusta causa non impeditus, per se ipse suos subditos ordinet; sed subditum orientalis ritus, sine apostolico indulto, licite ordinare non potest.

[81] Cœlestinus (III) Hidronensi archiepiscopo. *De presbytero latino a græco episcopo ordinato. Ne fiant commixtiones rituum in Ordinibus conferendis.* — Pontificia Commissio ad redigendum Codicem Iuris Canonici Orientalis, *Fontes*, Series III, Vol. I *Acta Romanorum Pontificum a S. Clemente I (an. c. 90) ad Cœlestinum III (+ 1198)* (Typis Polyglottis Vaticanis, 1943), n. 400 (the date of this letter is laid in the Pontificate of Pope Celestine III).

[82] Cinthio, tit. Sancti Laurenti in Lucina presbytero Cardinali, Apostolicæ Sedis Legato. *De ordinatione clericorum græcorum, latino episcopo subiectorum, ab episcopo græco.* — Pontificia Commissio ad redigendum Codicem Iuris Canonici Orientalis, *Fontes*,

of May 26, 1742, forbade for the future any such ordination without the special permission of the Holy See.[83] Further, he provided in the same Constitution that in case Italo-Albanians are ordained by Latin bishops without the permission of the Holy See, they thereby are incorporated in the Latin rite, and cannot return to their native Italo-Albanian rite without a dispensation from the Holy See.[84] Thus the Oriental candidate subject to the Latin ordinary was to be ordained by the local Latin ordinary with an apostolic indult,[85] and the same rule now obtains in view of the law enacted in canon 955.

At times an apostolic indult may be given to the Latin ordinary to send his Oriental subject to an Oriental bishop of a different rite for ordination.[86] In fact, it is always possible for the Latin ordinary, when he possesses an apostolic indult for the proper authorization, to send the dimissorial letters even with reference to his Oriental subject to another bishop in order to instruct the latter to ordain this subject.[87] If the Latin ordinary should send his Oriental subject to be ordained by an Oriental bishop of a rite identical with the recipients, then an indult from the Holy See would not be necessary.[88] The reason is obvious, for then the Oriental ordinand would be ordained

---

Series III, Vol. II *Acta Innocentii PP. III (1198-1216)* (e registris Vaticanis aliisque eruit, introductione auxit, notisque illustravit P. Theodosius Haluščynskyj, Typis Polyglottis Vaticanis, 1944), Pars I, n. 18.

[83] § VII, n. XX — *Fontes*, n. 328.

[84] § VII, n. XXIV — *Fontes*, n. 328; cf. Petrani, *De Relatione Iuridica inter Diversos Ritus in Ecclesia Catholica*, p. 92.

[85] Papp-Szilágyi, *Enchiridion Iuris Ecclesiæ Orientalis Catholicæ*, p. 240; *Fonti*, II, 397.

[86] Cappello, *Tractatus Canonico-Moralis de Sacramentis* (Vol. II, Pars III, 1935) Vol. II, Pars III, n. 339 (hereafter cited *De Sacramentis*, Vol. II, Pars III).

[87] Canon 961. Litteræ dimissoriæ mitti possunt ab Episcopo proprio, etiam Cardinali Episcopo suburbicario, ad quemlibet Episcopum, communionem cum Sede Apostolica habentem, excepto tantum, citra apostolicum indultum, Episcopo ritus diversi a ritu promovendi.

[88] Canon 961; cf. Cappello, *De Sacramentis*, Vol. II, Pars III, n. 343; Jone, *Gesetzbuch des kanonischen Rechtes*, II, 166.

by a bishop of his own rite, the dimissorial letters being furnished by the proper ordinary of the ordinand.

The Code of Canon Law gives the religious superior the permission to send his candidates for ordination with proper dimissorial letters to another bishop, if the bishop of the diocese be of a different rite.[89]

II. THE ORIENTAL CANDIDATE FOR ORDINATION

The Latin ordinary's power with regard to the ordination of his Oriental subjects is restricted in certain things. In the requirements of proper age, of the requisite good moral character, and of the demanded degree of knowledge, the Oriental candidates follow the prescriptions of their own rite in the measure and to the extent in which they exist.[90]

Irregularities exist also in Oriental law, and Oriental candidates subject to Latin ordinaries are bound by these. Their enumeration differs greatly among the various rites.[91]

III. THE RITE OF ORDINATION

Here there is question only of the ordination of an Oriental candidate by a Latin bishop authorized with an apostolic indult to confer the ordination. The Latin ordinary follows strictly the ceremonies of ordination of his own rite.[92] If the Oriental candidate has already received some orders from an Oriental bishop, then the Latin ordinary must supply any orders missing according to the

---

[89] Canon *966*. Tunc tantum Superior religiosus ad alium Episcopum litteras dimissorias mittere potest, cum Episcopus diœcesanus licentiam dederit, aut sit diversi ritus, . . . Cf. Dausend, *Das interrituelle Recht im Codex Iuris Canonici*, p. 114.

[90] Cappello, *De Sacramentis*, Vol. II, Pars III, n. 738; *Fonti*, XII, nn. 1026, 1035; *Fonti*, XV, nn. 589, 590, 598; *Fonti*, Serie II, Fasc. VII, nn. 726-728; *Fonti*, Serie II, Fasc. XVII, 62.

[91] Cappello, *De Sacramentis*, Vol. II, Pars III, n. 739; *Synodus Sciarfensis Syrorum*, pp. 155-160; *Fonti*, VII, n. 584; *Fonti*, Serie II, Fasc. VII, nn. 729, 730, 732, 733.

[92] Canon 1002; cf. *Fonti*, XII, n. 1028; Cappello, *De Sacramentis*, Vol. II, Pars III, n. 747.

Latin rite.[93] The supplementing of orders applies only to those orders not in existence in the various Oriental rites, and not to those contained implicitly in the orders already conferred.[94]

The Latin ordinary ordaining his Oriental candidates follows the interritual prescription of the Code of Canon Law for the time of ordination.[95] Oriental candidates for major orders subject to the Latin ordinaries may be ordained according to the provision of canon 981, *titulo servitii diœcesis,* which is also admitted in Oriental law.[96] As for the records and certificates of ordination the Latin ordinary follows the prescriptions of the Code of Canon Law.[97]

Even though Orientals may be permitted to marry before ordination according to their own law, the Latin ordinary, in order to forestall any possible moral bewilderment or even scandal among the people, and following also the letter of the Sacred Congregation for the Propagation of the Faith addressed to the Archbishop of Baltimore on May 10, 1892, should ordain only celibate Oriental candidates to the priesthood in the United States.[98]

---

[93] Canon 1004. Si quis, ritu orientali ad aliquos ordines iam promotus, a Sede Apostolica indultum obtinuerit superiores ordines suscipiendi ritu latino, debet prius ritu latino recipere ordines quos ritu orientali non receperit.

[94] Dausend, *Das interrituelle Recht im Codex Iuris Canonici,* pp. 104-105; Petrani, *De Relatione Iuridica inter Diversos Ritus in Ecclesia Catholica,* p. 93; Cappello, *De Sacramentis,* Vol. II, Pars III, n. 729; Papp-Szilágyi, *Enchiridion Iuris Ecclesiæ Orientalis Catholicæ,* pp. 239-240; Beste, *Introductio in Codicem,* p. 540; *Fonti,* X, n. 868; *Synodus Sciarfensis Syrorum,* pp. 132-133. Only the Armenians have the same number of orders as the Latins.

[95] Canon 1006, § 5. Reprobatur consuetudo contra ordinationum tempora præcedentibus paragraphis præscripta; quæ servanda quoque sunt, cum Episcopus latini ritus ordinat ex apostolico indulto clericum ritus orientalis aut contra. Cf. Dausend, *Das interrituelle Recht im Codex Iuris Canonici,* p. 105; Petrani, *De Relatione Iuridica inter Diversos Ritus in Ecclesia Catholica,* p. 93.

[96] Canon 981; Cappello, *De Sacramentis,* Vol. II, Pars III, n. 742.

[97] Canons 1010-1011.

[98] *AKKR,* LXVIII (1892), 442; S. C. pro Eccl. Or., decr. *Qua sollerti,* 23 dec. 1929 — *AAS,* XXII (1930), 99-105; Bouscaren, *The Canon Law Digest,* I, 17-24; Duskie, *The Canonical Status of the Orientals in the United States,* pp. 31-32.

ARTICLE 5. THE SACRAMENT OF MATRIMONY[99]

The Orientals subject to the Latin ordinaries in the United States, with reference to the administration of the sacrament of matrimony follow the prescriptions of their own particular law. The Latin ordinary's intervention will be called upon by his Oriental subjects principally in cases of dispensations from matrimonial impediments, or in the convalidations of their marriages. For a better understanding of the problems facing the Latin ordinary in this regard, a few summary remarks concerning the prescriptions of the particular law of the various Oriental rites, and also concerning the application of several canons of the Code of Canon Law, will be in order here.

I. PRELIMINARIES TO THE SACRAMENT OF MATRIMONY

Oriental law, like the Code of Canon Law, admits betrothals, with the distinction, however, that in the various Oriental rites they still constitute an impediment to marriage.[100] It is only natural that an investigation of the freedom of the parties for marriage must be made also by Oriental priests.[101]

The publication of the banns before marriage is regulated in the various Oriental rites similarly as in the Latin Church. The bishop has the power to dispense from one or all three of these publications according to his prudent judgment. This power the Latin ordinary also may use in favor of his Oriental subjects, inasmuch as the exercise

[99] For a more detailed treatment confer Dauvillier-De Clercq, *Le Marriage en Droit Canonique Oriental* (Paris: Librarie de Recueil Sirey, 1936).

[100] Canon 1017; Cappello, *Tractatus Canonico-Moralis de Sacramentis* (Vol. III, 3 ed., 1933), Vol. III, n. 895 (hereafter cited as *De Sacramentis,* III); Papp-Szilágyi, *Enchiridion Iuris Ecclesiæ Orientalis Catholicæ,* pp. 244-245; Dauvillier-De Clercq, *Le Marriage en Droit Canonique Oriental,* pp. 32-39.

[101] Canon 1020; *Fonti,* XV, n. 315; *Fonti,* Serie II, Fasc. VII, nn. 743, 808; *Fonti,* Serie II, Fasc. XVII, 64.

of this power is simply a matter of prudent supervision over his subjects.[102]

II. THE IMPEDIMENTS TO MARRIAGE

Most of the matrimonial impediments in the various Oriental rites are the same and closely resemble those of the Latin Church. In their extension they vary, however, not only from those of the Latin rite, but they differ also in the various Oriental rites. Some impediments of the Oriental law are the same as were those of the Latin Church before the enactment of the Code of Canon Law. The impedient impediments which seem to exist in most of the Oriental rites are the following: betrothals,[103] mixed religion,[104] sacred or forbidden times,[105] the simple vow of chastity,[106] and the prohibition by the Church.[107] Lack

---

[102] Canon 1022; *Fonti,* X, nn. 960-969; *Fonti,* XII, nn. 1204-1212, 1214-1218; *Fonti,* Serie II, Fasc. VII, nn. 740, 746, 759.

[103] Only those entered into formally. Cappello, *De Sacramentis,* III, nn. 898-900; Milasch, *Das Kirchenrecht der Morgenländischen Kirche* (translated into German by Dr. Alexander Pessić, Mostar: Pacher & Kisić, 1905), pp. 587-590; *Synodus Sciarfensis Syrorum,* pp. 161, 173; *Fonti,* Serie II, Fasc. VII, n. 781.

[104] Canons 1060-1064; Cappello, *op. cit.,* III, nn. 898-900; Milasch, *op. cit.,* pp. 621, 643-645; *Fonti,* XV, n. 269; *Fonti,* Serie II, Fasc. VII, n. 766; *Synodus Sciarfensis Syrorum,* p. 174.

[105] Understood are certain times such as Lent, days of fast, and feast days according to the prescriptions of each rite, on which the solemn administration of the sacrament of matrimony is prohibited. Cappello, *loc. cit.;* Papp-Szilágyi, *Enchiridion Iuris Ecclesiæ Orientalis Catholicæ,* p. 278; Vering, *Lehrbuch des katholischen, orientalischen und protestantischen Kirchenrechts,* p. 924; *Synodus Sciarfensis Syrorum,* p. 173.

[106] For some Oriental rites also the vow of entering religion and of not contracting marriage. Cappello, *De Sacramentis,* III, nn. 898-900; cf. Dauvillier-De Clercq, *Le Marriage en Droit Canonique Oriental,* p. 182; *Fonti,* X, n. 1235; *Synodus Sciarfensis Syrorum,* p. 173.

[107] Under this title the prohibition of parents and guardians may be included. Compared with this impediment may be also the prohibitive power of the Latin ordinary according to canon 1039. Cf. Cappello, *De Sacramentis,* Vol. III, nn. 898-900; Papp-Szilágyi, *Enchiridion Iuris Ecclesiæ Orientalis Catholicæ,* p. 278; Dauvillier-De Clercq, *Le Marriage en Droit Canonique Oriental,* p. 157; Milasch, *Das Kirchenrecht der Morgenländischen Kirche,* pp. 620-621; Vering, *Lehrbuch des katholischen, orientalischen und protestantischen Kirchenrechts,* p. 922; *Fonti,* X, n. 644; *Fonti,* XV, n. 267; *Synodus Sciarfensis Syrorum,* p. 175.

of required age, fourteen for men and twelve for women, is an impedient impediment for the Maronites, and requires a dispensation from the bishop even when the prospective contracting parties certainly possess the capacity for marriage.[108] *Catechismus* is an impedient impediment peculiar to the Maronites.[109]

The diriment impediments of impotence and of a previous marriage bond oblige all Catholic Orientals in virtue of the natural and the positive divine law respectively.[110] The other diriment impediments among the various Oriental rites whose members are subject to the Latin ordinaries in the United States are the following: age,[111] disparity of cult,[112] holy orders,[113] solemn religious

---

[108] *Fonti,* XII, nn. 874, 893; *Collectio Lacensis,* II, 169, b; cf. Bouscaren, *The Canon Law Digest,* I, 5; Cappello, *De Sacramentis,* III, n. 898.

[109] It arises when baptism has been conferred privately, and exists between the person baptized and those who bring him for the supplying of the ceremonies of baptism. Cf. *Fonti,* XII, n. 197; Cappello, *loc. cit.*

[110] Canons 1068 and 1069; cf. Cappello, *De Sacramentis,* III, nn. 904-905; Papp-Szilágyi, *Enchiridion Iuris Ecclesiæ Orientalis Catholicæ,* pp. 247-248, 251-253; *Fonti,* X, n. 645; *Synodus Sciarfensis Syrorum,* p. 177.

[111] Among most of the rites the age is fourteen for boys and twelve for girls. The rule *nisi malitia suppleat ætatem* is still in effect in Oriental law. Cappello, *op. cit.,* III, n. 902; Papp-Szilágyi, *op. cit.,* p. 248; Vering, *Lehrbuch des katholischen, orientalischen und protestantischen Kirchenrechts,* p. 889; Dauvillier-De Clercq, *Le Marriage en Droit Canonique Oriental,* pp. 158-161; *Fonti,* X, n. 47; *Fonti,* XV, n. 261; *Fonti,* Serie II, Fasc. VII, n. 770; *Fonti,* Serie II, Fasc. XVII, 64; *Synodus Sciarfensis Syrorum,* p. 176.

[112] This impediment exists in the manner in which it existed in the Latin Church before the enactment of the Code of Canon Law, i.e., between baptized persons and the non-baptized. Cappello, *De Sacramentis,* III, n. 906; Papp-Szilágyi, *op. cit.,* pp. 257-259; Vering, *op. cit.,* p. 915; Dauvillier-De Clercq, *op. cit.,* pp. 170-171; *Synodus Sciarfensis Syrorum,* p. 181.

[113] While married candidates may be permitted to receive major orders, except in the Armenian rite, candidates for ordinations in the United States are to be celibates, as explained in the previous article. It is also the more probable opinion that marriages contracted after the reception of major orders are invalid. Cf. Cappello, *De Sacramentis,* III, nn. 907-908; *Fonti,* XII, nn. 877, 878; Benedictus XIV, const. *Etsi pastoralis,* 26 maii 1742, § VII, n. XXVII — *Fontes,* n. 328; *Fonti,* Serie II, Fasc. VII, n. 783; *Synodus Sciarfensis Syrorum,* p. 177; Dauvillier-De Clercq, *Le Marriage en Droit Canonique Oriental,* p. 174.

profession,[114] abduction,[115] crime,[116] consanguinity,[117] affinity,[118] public propriety,[119] spiritual relationship,[120] and legal adoption.[121]

The canons of the Code of Canon Law on error, the marriage consent, and on conditions imposed on the matrimonial consent apply by their very nature also to

---

[114] Cappello, *op. cit.*, III, n. 912; Dauvillier-De Clercq, *op. cit.*, pp. 179-183; Papp-Szilágyi, *Enchiridion Iuris Ecclesiæ Orientalis Catholicæ*, p. 256; Vering, *Lehrbuch des katholischen, orientalischen und protestantischen Kirchenrechts*, p. 908; *Fonti*, X, nn. 1233, 1234; *Fonti*, XII, n. 877; *Fonti*, Serie II, Fasc. VII, n. 782; *Synodus Sciarfensis Syrorum*, p. 177.

[115] Cappello, *op. cit.*, III, n. 914; Dauvillier-De Clercq, *op. cit.*, pp. 185-190; Papp-Szilágyi, *op. cit.*, pp. 250-251; *Fonti*, X, n. 978; *Fonti*, XII, n. 1219; *Fonti*, IV, 267; *Synodus Sciarfensis Syrorum*, p. 181.

[116] Not in existence in the Melkite rite. Cappello, *De Sacramentis*, III, n. 915; Papp-Szilágyi, *Enchiridion Iuris Ecclesiæ Orientalis Catholicæ*, p. 272; Dauvillier-De Clercq, *Le Marriage en Droit Canonique Oriental*, pp. 192-193; Vering, *Lehrbuch des katholischen, orientalischen und protestantischen Kirchenrechts*, p. 911; *Synodus Sciarfensis Syrorum*, p. 182; *Fonti*, XII, nn. 420, 403; *Fonti*, Serie II, Fasc. VII, n. 779; in the Rumanian rite only the killing of a spouse when effected by mutual conspiracy and when accompanied with the intention of marrying as entertained by at least one of the parties: "Coniugicidium ex communi conspiratione et cum intentione contrahendi saltem ab uno habita matrimonium dirimit." — *Fonti*, X, n. 437.

[117] In the direct line the extension of the impediment is the same as in the Code of Canon Law, canon 1076, § 1. In the collateral line the extension of the impediment differs in the various rites. Cappello, *op. cit.*, III, n. 917; Dauvillier-De Clercq, *op. cit.*, pp. 127-136; *Fonti*, X, n. 314; *Fonti*, XII, nn. 405, 406; *Fonti*, Serie II, Fasc. VII, n. 788; *Fonti*, Serie II, Fasc. XV, 174-176; *Synodus Sciarfensis Syrorum*, pp. 178-180.

[118] It exists in Oriental law as it existed in the Latin Church before the enactment of the Code of Canon Law. Cappello, *De Sacramentis*, III, n. 918; Dauvillier-De Clercq, *Le Marriage en Droit Canonique Oriental*, p. 146; *Fonti*, X, nn. 48-50; *Fonti*, XII, nn. 54-56; *Fonti*, Serie II, Fasc. VII, n. 795; *Synodus Sciarfensis Syrorum*, pp. 180-181.

[119] It arises as it formerly arose in the Latin Church before the enactment of the law of the present Code of Canon Law. Cappello, *op. cit.*, III, n. 919; Papp-Szilágyi, *Enchiridion Iuris Ecclesiæ Orientalis Catholicæ*, pp. 271-272; *Fonti*, X, n. 979; *Synodus Sciarfensis Syrorum*, p. 181.

[120] It arises in connection both with baptism and with confirmation. Its extension varies in the different Oriental rites. Cappello, *op. cit.*, III, n. 920; Papp-Szilágyi, *op. cit.*, pp. 266-267; Dauvillier-De Clercq, *Le Marriage en Droit Canonique Oriental*, pp. 146-153; *Synodus Sciarfensis Syrorum*, p. 180; cf. Chapter VII, Article 1.

[121] It is a diriment impediment in all Oriental rites. Its extension, however, varies. Cappello, *De Sacramentis*, III, n. 921; Papp-Szilágyi, *Enchiridion Iuris Ecclesiæ Orientalis Catholicæ*, p. 268; Dauvillier-De Clercq, *Le Marriage en Droit Canonique Oriental*, pp. 153-156; *Fonti*, X, n. 313; *Fonti*, XII, nn. 282-283; *Fonti*, Serie II, Fasc. VII, n. 792; *Synodus Sciarfensis Syrorum*, p. 180.

Orientals. At times a defective matrimonial consent is better known among the various Oriental rites as the impediment of fear and force.[122]

III. THE FORM OF MARRIAGE

It is hoped that the prospective new Code for the Orientals will settle the difficulties and doubts about the form of marriage among the various Oriental rites. Those Orientals who live in the United States under the jurisdiction of the Latin ordinaries apparently use the following form in the sacrament of matrimony.

1. *The Syrians.* They appear to require the blessing of the priests for the licitness of a marriage.[123]

2. *The Maronites.* Those living in the United States are probably not bound by any particular form.[124]

3. *The Armenians.* For licitness it is required that their marriages be celebrated before a priest.[125]

4. *The Chaldeans.* The blessing of the priest before witnesses is usually required for the licitness of their marriages.[126]

---

[122] Papp-Szilágyi, *op. cit.*, pp. 249-250; Vering, *Lehrbuch des katholischen, orientalischen und protestantischen Kirchenrechts*, p. 885; *Fonti*, X, n. 1226; *Fonti*, XII, nn. 1505, 1506; *Fonti*, Serie II, Fasc. VII, n. 764; *Synodus Sciarfensis Syrorum*, p. 176.

[123] *Synodus Sciarfensis Syrorum*, pp. 189-190; cf. Cappello, *De Sacramentis*, III, n. 924; Duskie, *The Canonical Status of the Orientals in the United States*, p. 157.

[124] See the private response of the Sacred Congregation for the Oriental Church on December 19, 1928, published in Bouscaren, *The Canon Law Digest*, I, 5 (not in the *AAS*); cf. Duskie, *op. cit.*, pp. 158-162.

[125] *Acta et Decreta Concilii Nationalis Armenorum Romæ habiti, an. 1911* (Romæ: Typis Polyglottis Vaticanis, 1913), n. 575; cf. Cappello, *De Sacramentis*, III, n. 925; Duskie, *The Canonical Status of the Orientals in the United States*, p. 158; Gulovich, "Matrimonial Laws of the Catholic Eastern Churches," — *The Jurist*, IV (1944), 216.

[126] The acts of the Chaldean Synod, held in 1853 with the authorization of the Holy See, though never approved, provide that marriages must be contracted in the presence of a priest and at least two witnesses: *Fonti*, Serie II, Fasc. XVII, 65; cf. *Fonti*, IV, 181; Duskie, *The Canonical Status of the Orientals in the United States*, p. 158.

5. *The Melkites.* No form seems to be required for the validity of their marriages.[127]

6. *The Rumanians.* For the validity of their marriages no form seems to be required, while for licitness the nuptial contracts must be entered into before the proper pastor, or before a priest with the permission of the proper pastor or the bishop, and before two or three witnesses.[128]

7. *The Russians.* At least for the licitness of their marriages the blessing of the proper pastor or of a delegated priest seems to be required. In case the contracting parties are of two different parishes the proper pastor is the pastor of the bridegroom.[129]

8. *The Italo-Albanians.* In virtue of the Constitution *Etsi pastoralis* of Pope Benedict XIV, issued on May 26, 1742, members of this rite who live in the United States of America are bound to the Tridentine form of marriage.[130]

In short, any specific juridical form for the contracting of marriage in the various Oriental rites under the jurisdiction of the Latin ordinaries in the United States does not seem to bind under pain of nullity with the exception of the Italo-Albanians.[131]

The canons of the Code of Canon Law on the dissolution, separation, and convalidation of marriages for the

---

[127] Cf. Bouscaren, *The Canon Law Digest,* I, 543; Vermeersch-Creusen, *Epitome Iuris Canonici* (5 ed., 3 vols., Mechliniæ-Romæ: H. Dessain, 1933-1936), II, n. 407; Dauvillier-De Clercq, *Le Marriage en Droit Canonique Oriental,* p. 46.

[128] *Fonti,* X, n. 752; Duskie, *The Canonical Status of the Orientals in the United States,* pp. 156-157; Dauvillier-De Clercq, *op. cit.,* pp. 45-46.

[129] *Fonti,* Serie II, Fasc. VII, nn. 754, 757-758, 805.

[130] § VIII, n. I — *Fontes,* n. 328; cf. Cappello, *De Sacramentis,* III, n. 925; Duskie, *The Canonical Status of the Orientals in the United States,* pp. 162-163. In Italy they are now definitely bound by the Latin form of the Code of Canon Law as explained in Chaper II, Article 1.

[131] Cf. also Gulovich, "The Principle underlying the validity of Oriental marriage law," — *The Jurist,* VI (1946), 39-49.

greater part and with proper restrictions are also applicable to Orientals, partly because the matter concerns faith and morals, partly because these canons treat certain principles of law, and also because without the observance of these canons by all the faithful public order could not be maintained.[132]

IV. DISPENSATIONS

It has already been stated that the Latin ordinary cannot dispense his Oriental subjects from matrimonial impediments in virtue of his quinquennial faculties, except those which emanate from the Holy Office and the Sacred Penitentiary. Simply in view of the fact that a Latin ordinary has Orientals as his subjects, it does not follow that he has the power peculiar to the office of an Oriental bishop, i.e., those powers which each particular Oriental rite attributes to the office of a bishop of that rite, and which powers are different from those attributed to the office of a Latin bishop. Hence the Latin ordinaries cannot grant those dispensations to his Oriental subjects which are peculiar to the Oriental rites and which are granted by an Oriental ordinary in virtue of the power given him by each particular rite.[133] However, the Latin ordinary can use the provisions of canons 1043 and 1045, § 1, in favor also of his Oriental subjects. In the same manner the Latin confessor may avail himself of the provisions of canons 1044 and 1045, § 3. Canons 15 and 209, as general principles of law and as regulations intended for the general good of souls, may be applied to the Orientals.[134]

---

[132] Dausend, *Das interrituelle Recht im Codex Iuris Canonici*, pp. 32-47; Cappello, *Summa Iuris Canonici*, I, n. 62; cf. Chapter V, Article 1.

[133] Cf. Chapter IV.

[134] Cappello, *De Sacramentis*, III, n. 923; Duskie, *The Canonical Status of the Orientals in the United States*, pp. 177-178.

V. SOME INTERRITUAL RELATIONS

Orientals when marrying Latins must observe the form of the Code of Canon Law.[135] If Orientals of different rites contract marriages among themselves, then these marriages are to be entered into in the rite and consequently also according to the form of the groom and before his pastor if no definite particular law of the one or the other of the represented rites prescribes any ruling to the contrary.[136]

However, the particular law of the Greek-Ruthenians in the United States demands that marriages between Greek-Ruthenians and the faithful of other rites be contracted with the observance of the form prescribed by the decree *Ne temere* before the pastor of the bride, except for a just reason and according to the prudent judgment, and with the consent of the ordinary of the place. Further, matrimonial dispensations for these marriages, when they are needed, must be asked of the ordinary of the bride.[137] Consequently, if a man of any of the Oriental rites whose members are subject to the Latin ordinaries in the United States marries a Ruthenian woman, then the marriage is to be celebrated before the competent Ruthenian pastor, and in case any dispensations are needed, they are to be obtained from the Ruthenian bishop.[138]

---

[135] Canon 1099, § 1, 3°; cf. Duskie, *op. cit.*, p. 169.

[136] Canon 1097, 2; cf. Duskie, *The Canonical Status of the Orientals in the United States*, p. 169; Herman, "Quibus normis matrimonium regatur quod inter fideles diversi ritus contrahitur," — *Analecta Gregoriana*, Vols. IX-X, *Miscellanea Vermeersch* (2 vols., Roma: Pontificia Universita Gregoriana, 1935), I, 241-253.

[137] S. C. pro Eccl. Or., decr. *Cum data fuerit*, 1 mart. 1929 — *AAS*, XXI (1929), 159; Bouscaren, *The Canon Law Digest*, I, 16; S. C. pro Eccl. Or., decr. *Per Decretum*, 23 nov. 1940 — *AAS*, XXXIII (1941), 27; Bouscaren, *The Canon Law Digest*, II, 7.

[138] Cf. Plöchl, "The change of rite *in matrimonio ineundo vel eo durante*," — *The Jurist*, VI (1946), 295-303.

Article 6. The Sacrament of Extreme Unction, Sacramentals, and Indulgences

I. THE SACRAMENT OF EXTREME UNCTION

The Latin ordinary's intervention in the administration of the sacrament of extreme unction by his Oriental priests will only seldom be called upon. Most of the Oriental priests according to the prescriptions of their rite bless the oil of the sick themselves.[139] However, the Maronites, the Syrians, and most probably also the Chaldeans use the oil blessed by their bishops, and the Armenians that blessed by their Patriarch.[140] Since the priests of these rites do not possess their own bishops or patriarchs in the United States, they will receive the oil of the sick from their own respective Latin ordinaries. Neither is the blessing of this oil on the part of the Latin ordinary a usurpation of the office of an Oriental bishop, since such a blessing is nothing peculiar to the office of an Oriental bishop and the Latin ordinary possesses the same power in virtue of his own office.

The right to administer the sacrament of extreme unction always belongs to the pastor of the place.[141] However, in a case of necessity Oriental priests may administer this sacrament to Latins with the presumed permission of the pastor, and likewise Latin priests may administer it to Orientals. In such cases the priest administering the sacrament follows his own rite, even though the subject be of

---

[139] Petrani, *De Relatione Iuridica inter Diversos Ritus in Ecclesia Catholica*, p. 90; Papp-Szilágyi, *Enchiridion Iuris Ecclesiæ Orientalis Catholicæ*, p. 237; Cappello, *Tractatus Canonico-Moralis de Sacramentis* (Vol. II, Pars II, 1932), Vol. II, Pars II, nn. 308-314; *Fonti*, X, n. 601; *Fonti*, XV, nn. 858-859.

[140] Cappello, *op. cit.*, Vol. II, Pars II, nn. 295-297; *Fonti*, XII, n. 670; *Synodus Sciarfensis Syrorum*, p. 123; *Fonti*, Serie II, Fasc. XVII, 61; *Acta et Decreta Concilii Nationalis Armenorum Romæ habiti, an. 1911*, p. 496.

[141] Canon 938; *Fonti*, X, n. 603; *Fonti*, XII, n. 677.

another.[142] Only in the ritual administration of this sacrament do Orientals differ from the Latins. The laws of the Code of Canon Law regarding the necessity of the reception of this sacrament, its minister, its subject, its repetition, and its conditional administration are also applicable to Orientals by their very nature.[143]

II. SACRAMENTALS

The Canons of the Code of Canon Law on the sacramentals are by their very nature also applicable to Orientals. However, the canons on exorcism are excluded since they are merely disciplinary in nature.[144] In the administration of the sacramentals the observance of the prescribed formulas by the minister is necessary not only for licitness but also for the validity of the sacramentals.[145]

III. INDULGENCES

Since by indulgences spiritual favors are granted for the general welfare of souls, they by their very nature rule out a distinction between Catholics of the Latin Church and those of the Oriental Church. All canons of the Code of Canon Law on indulgences, except what is foreign and unknown to the various Oriental rites, are also applicable to Orientals.[146]

Practically, then, all indulgences granted by the Pope through a universal decree may also be gained by Orien-

---

[142] Cappello, *De Sacramentis*, Vol. II, Pars II, nn. 319-321; Dausend, *Das interrituelle Recht im Codex Iuris Canonici*, pp. 103-104; Duskie, *The Canonical Status of the Orientals in the United States*, pp. 147-148.

[143] Dausend, *op. cit.*, pp. 36-37; cf. Chapter V, Article 1; *Fonti*, XII, nn. 674, 676, 686; *Fonti*, II, 239, 241; *Fonti*, X, n. 606; *Fonti*, Serie II, Fasc. VII, n. 722; *Synodus Sciarfensis Syrorum*, pp. 123-124; Cappello, *De Sacramentis*, Vol. II, Pars II, n. 310.

[144] Cf. Chapter V, Article 1.

[145] Canon 1148; Dausend, *Das interrituelle Recht im Codex Iuris Canonici*, pp. 92-93.

[146] Cf. Chapter V, Article 1; Duskie, *The Canonical Status of the Orientals in the United States*, p. 143.

tals.[147] Likewise Orientals subject to Latin ordinaries seem to be able to gain the indulgences which Latin residential bishops can impart according to canons 349 and 914, and with the enlargement granted by Pope Pius XII on June 8, 1942.[148]

---

[147] S. Pœnit. (Sect. de Indulg.), 7 iul. 1917 — *Fontes*, n. 6450; *AAS*, IX (1917), 399; Duskie, *op. cit.*, p. 143; Cappello, *De Sacramentis*, Vol. II, Pars I, n. 1049; S. C. pro Eccl. Or., notificatio, 10 aug. 1943 — *AAS*, XXXVI (1944), 47-59.

[148] S. Pœnit. 20 iul. 1942 — *AAS*, XXXIV (1942), 240; Bouscaren, *The Canon Law Digest*, II, 221-222.

CHAPTER VIII

MISCELLANEA

Article 1. Sacred Places and Times

I. SACRED PLACES

The erection of churches in a diocese lies entirely within the competence of the proper ordinary.[1] If the erection of a church, destined to serve an Oriental rite under the jurisdiction of the Latin ordinary, is warranted, then the Latin ordinary is also the one who blesses or consecrates it. However, prudence will dictate that the interior of this Oriental church be in conformity with the usages of the respective rite and designed to make the execution of all the ceremonies according to the Oriental rite possible. For the support of the church, in fact for all acquisitions and for the protection of church property, Oriental churches are governed by local legislation. The Church in such matters follows the prescriptions of the civil law, as long as there is no opposition to divine positive law or canonical norms.[2]

The norms with reference to the violation of an Oriental church subject to the Latin ordinary's jurisdiction are, however, those which obtain in the particular rite. These norms differ somewhat from those of the Code of Canon Law.[3]

The right to bury his subjects belongs to the Oriental priest caring for his faithful in the same manner as it belongs to the Latin pastor according to the Code of

[1] Canon 1162.

[2] S. C. pro Eccl. Or., decr. *Qua sollerti,* 23 dec. 1929 — *AAS,* XXII (1930), 104; Bouscaren, *The Canon Law Digest,* I, 23; canon 1529; Duskie, *The Canonical Status of the Orientals in the United States,* p. 68.

[3] *Synodus Sciarfensis Syrorum,* p. 263; *Fonti,* X, n. 321; *Fonti,* XII, n. 513.

Canon Law. If Orientals in Latin territory choose a place of burial, or in consequence of necessitating circumstances receive burial, in Latin cemeteries, then in this regard they follow the laws of the Code of Canon Law.[4] In the United States Orientals subject to Latin ordinaries are usually buried in Latin cemeteries. In these cases, it is the Oriental priest caring for his flock who, after the services in the Oriental church, will officiate at the burial services in the Latin cemeteries.

The ceremonies for burial will be according to the ritual of each rite. Likewise the norms governing the denial of ecclesiastical burial will be those of each rite, since they are personal laws. However, they are similar to those of the Code of Canon Law.[5]

II. SACRED TIMES

The Latin ordinary's jurisdiction over his Oriental subjects is restricted by the prescriptions of the various Oriental rites concerning their feast days and days of fast and of abstinence. Orientals celebrate the feast days of our Lord, of the Blessed Virgin Mary, and of the Saints according to the prescriptions of their own rite, some following the Julian, some the Gregorian calendar.[6]

Canon 1249 is interritual in its legislation, stating that the obligation of attending Holy Mass on the prescribed days may be satisfied through an attendance at Mass in whatever rite it be celebrated.[7]

---

[4] Cf. Petrani, *De Relatione Iuridica inter Diversos Ritus in Ecclesia Catholica*, p. 60.

[5] Cf. Chapter V, Article 1; Papp-Szilágyi, *Enchiridion Iuris Ecclesiæ Orientalis Catholicæ*, p. 303; *Fonti*, X, nn. 1097-1100; *Fonti*, XII, n. 1403; *Fonti*, Serie II, Fasc. VII, nn. 768-769; *Synodus Sciarfensis Syrorum*, p. 128.

[6] Petrani, *De Relatione Iuridica inter Diversos Ritus in Ecclesia Catholica*, pp. 101-106; *Fonti*, X, nn. 460-461; *Fonti*, XII, nn. 458-463; *Fonti*, XV, n. 231; *Fonti*, Serie II, Fasc. VII, n. 974, note 1; *Fonti*, Serie II, Fasc. XVII, 69-72; Papp-Szilágyi, *op. cit.*, pp. 294-299; *Synodus Sciarfensis Syrorum*, pp. 62-67.

[7] Canon 1249. Legi de audiendo Sacro satisfacit qui Missæ adest quocumque catholico ritu celebretur, sub dio aut in quacumque ecclesia . . .

Concerning fasts and abstinence the Orientals living in the United States and Canada may follow the prescriptions of their own rite, or they may also, in virtue of an indult granted by the Holy Father, follow the Latin rite.[8]

ARTICLE 2. DIVINE WORSHIP AND THE TEACHING AUTHORITY OF THE CHURCH

As a general principle Orientals subject to the Latin ordinaries follow the prescriptions of their own particular law in the matter of divine worship. The only canons of the Code of Canon Law on divine worship applicable to Orientals are those of a general nature.[9] In these cases the Oriental law is also the same. Such canons are those which regulate the cult that is due to God, to the Blessed Virgin, and to the saints,[10] and which deal with the veneration of the saints,[11] sacred images and relics,[12] and sacred processions.[13]

The law which prohibits Catholics from participating in non-Catholic worship applies to Orientals by its very nature, and the same norms exist also in Oriental law.[14]

Orientals are affected neither by the norms of the Code of Canon Law on the custody of the Holy Eucharist, nor by the Instruction of the Sacred Congregation of the Sac-

---

[8] Thus stated in a private reply from the Sacred Congregation for the Oriental Church on December 19, 1928, not published in the *AAS*, but to be found in Bouscaren, *The Canon Law Digest*, I, 4-5; cf. Bastnagel, "The Maronite Law of Abstinence," — *The Jurist*, III (1943), 145-149; S. C. de Prop. Fide, 10 mart. 1760 — *Collectanea*, n. 426.

[9] Cf. Chapter V, Article 1.

[10] Canon 1255; *Fonti*, X, n. 44.

[11] Canon 1276; *Fonti*, XII, n. 423; *Synodus Sciarfensis Syrorum*, p. 24; Petrani, *De Relatione Iuridica inter Diversos Ritus in Ecclesia Catholica*, pp. 101-102.

[12] Canons 1279; 1283, § 1; 1284, 1287; *Fonti*, XII, nn. 1299-1305; *Synodus Sciarfensis Syrorum*, pp. 25-26.

[13] Canon 1290; *Fonti*, Serie II, Fasc. VII, nn. 917-918; *Synodus Sciarfensis Syrorum*, pp. 50-52.

[14] Canon 1258; *Fonti*, X, nn. 335-336; *Fonti*, XII, nn. 294-297; *Fonti*, XV, n. 114.

raments on May 26, 1938, on the same matter, for they are not bound by the disciplinary laws enacted for the Latin Church. Consequently they follow the prescriptions of their own rites in this regard.[15] However, for Orientals subject to the Latin ordinary's jurisdiction the permission of the Latin ordinary would be necessary for them in the matter of the exposition of and benediction with the Blessed Sacrament, as the permission of their own ordinary is also commonly required today among many Oriental rites.[16]

Practically all the canons of the Code of Canon Law on vows and oaths by their very nature apply also to Orientals, and consequently the Latin ordinary can dispense also his Oriental subjects from non-reserved vows.[17]

As a matter for properly safeguarding faith and morals Orientals are bound by most canons of the Code of Canon Law concerning the prohibition of books, and also by the decrees of the Holy Office through which certain books and papers are condemned.[18]

No special mention will be made of processes for Orientals, since those who are subject to the Latin ordinaries in the United States will have to bring their petitions and cases to a Latin tribunal, which of course is bound in the conduct of its procedure by the canons of the Code of Canon Law.[19]

---

[15] Canons 1265-1275; S. C. Sacramentis, 26 maii 1938 — *AAS*, XXX (1938), 198-207; Bouscaren, *The Canon Law Digest*, II, 377-388; *Fonti*, XII, n. 628; *Fonti*, XV, n. 215; *Synodus Sciarfensis Syrorum*, p. 98; Cappello, *De Sacramentis*, I, n. 861.

[16] Cappello, *De Sacramentis*, I, n. 862; *Fonti*, XII, n. 626; *Synodus Sciarfensis Syrorum*, p. 99.

[17] Canon 1313; cf. Chapter V, Article 1.

[18] S. C. pro Eccl. Or., declar. 26 maii 1928 — *AAS*, XX (1928), 195; Bouscaren, *The Canon Law Digest*, I, 685; S. C. pro Eccl. Or., declar. (no date given), — *AAS*, XXXVI (1944), 25; Dausend, *Das interrituelle Recht im Codex Iuris Canonici*, p. 26; cf. *Synodus Sciarfensis Syrorum*, p. 227; cf. Chapter V, Article 1.

[19] Cf. Herman, "De Ritu in Iure Canonico," — *Orientalia Christiana*, XXXII (1933), 156; Duskie, *The Canonical Status of the Orientals in the United States*, p. 65.

Article 3. Delinquencies and Penalties

Since Orientals under the jurisdiction of the Latin ordinaries in the United States are subject to the particular laws of the diocese, they are consequently bound by any episcopal reservation of sins or censures existing in the diocese.[20] Further, they remain always subject to any reservation existing in their own particular law.[21] Even though they have been placed under the jurisdiction of the Latin ordinaries, they thereby are not generally bound by the reservations of censures enacted in the Code of Canon Law.[22]

The Constitution *Apostolicæ Sedis,* issued by Pope Pius IX (1846-1878) on October 12, 1869,[23] did not make any innovations for Orientals with regard to censures and their reservations.[24] But Orientals were declared subject to the censures of the common law concerning the faith, and in matters which implied a declaration of the natural and positive divine law.[25] This norm is applicable also now to the censures contained in the Code of Canon Law.[26]

Further, the penal sanctions contained in canons 2320, 2341, § 1, 2367, and 2369 of the Code of Canon Law, by which certain crimes are punished with a *latæ sententiæ* excommunication which for its absolution is reserved in a most special manner to the Holy See, in view of the extraordinary gravity of these crimes, extend to the universal Church including the Catholics of the Oriental

[20] Canons 2220, 2247; Duskie, *The Canonical Status of the Orientals in the United States,* p. 138.

[21] Cappello, *Tractatus Canonico-Moralis de Censuris* (2 ed., Taurinorum Augustæ: Marietti, 1925), n. 22.

[22] Duskie, *op. cit.,* p. 137.

[23] *Fontes,* n. 552.

[24] S. C. de Prop. Fide, litt. encycl. 6 aug. 1885, ad 1 — *Fontes,* n. 4910.

[25] S. C. de Prop. Fide, litt. encycl. 6 aug. 1885, ad 2 — *Fontes,* n. 4910; Cappello, *Tractatus Canonico-Moralis de Censuris,* n. 22.

[26] Duskie, *The Canonical Status of the Orientals in the United States,* p. 29.

rites. Cognizance of these crimes, as regards the internal forum, is reserved to the Sacred Penitentiary, and as regards the external forum, to the Holy Office.[27]

Concerning the absolution of the censures to which Orientals under the jurisdiction of the Latin ordinary may be subject, the Latin ordinary can absolve them from the censures reserved to himself. From those censures by which Orientals are bound by the Code of Canon Law according to the above mentioned norms, he can absolve according to his quinquennial faculties given him by the Holy Office and the Sacred Penitentiary.

From the reservation to which Orientals are bound according to the prescriptions of their own particular law he cannot in general absolve; he can grant absolution only in so far as he is given competence to do so through the faculties of the Holy Office and of the Sacred Penitentiary. Otherwise he cannot absolve from the latter reservations, since the power to do so was not shared with him through the fact simply that these Orientals were placed under his care. He can obtain this power, however, from the Sacred Congregation for the Oriental Church in the measure in which its use will prove feasible. The law of canons 882, 2252, and 2254 of the Code of Canon Law is applicable also to Orientals, since it was enacted for the general welfare of souls of all Catholics alike.[28]

---

[27] S. C. S. Off., decr., 21 iul. 1934—*AAS*, XXVI (1934), 550; Bouscaren, *The Canon Law Digest*, II, 577; cf. Dausend, *Das interrituelle Recht im Codex Iuris Canonici*, pp. 21-22; Jone, *Gesetzbuch des kanonischen Rechtes*, I, 15.

[28] Cf. Chapter V, Article 1.

Appendix I

THE CATHOLICS OF THE ORIENTAL CHURCH

The following is a summary of the various Oriental rites whose members could become subject to the Latin ordinaries.[1]

Division of the Catholic Orientals

I. Alexandrian Discipline:
   1. Copts
   2. Ethiopians

II. Antiochene Discipline:
   1. Syrians
   2. Maronites
   3. Malankarese

III. Armenian Discipline

IV. Chaldean Discipline:
   1. Chaldeans
   2. Malabarese

V. Byzantine Discipline:
   1. Albanians
   2. Bulgarians
   3. Georgians
   4. Greeks
   5. Hungarians
   6. Yugoslavs
   7. Melkites
   8. Rumanians
   9. Russians
   10. Ruthenians
   11. Italo-Albanians

A few remarks about each rite of the five disciplines are here in order.

The *Copts* are of Egyptian nationality. They converted from Monophysitism. Although their legates signed an act of union at the Council of Florence (1438-1445), and though another unsuccessful attempt at reunion was made in 1594, their final union with Rome dates from 1741. At present they have two episcopal sees with an Apostolic Administrator as their head. They number about 30,000 to 35,000 Catholics.

The *Ethiopians* are members of what may be called a sister church of the Coptic rite. They live mainly in Ethiopia and Eritrea. In spite of

---

[1] For more detailed information about these rites confer *Fonti*, VIII; *Statistica;* Fortescue, *The Uniate Eastern Churches* (Italo-Greeks and Melkites only); Fortescue, *The Lesser Eastern Churches* (London: Catholic Truth Society, 1913); Attwater, *The Catholic Eastern Churches;* Liturgical Arts Society, *The Eastern Branches of the Catholic Church* (New York: Longmans, Green and Co., 1938).

many missionary attempts, it is only since 1839 that one may speak of some church organization as existing among them. The ordinariate of Eritrea, established in 1930 with its residence at Asmara, counts about 30,000 faithful of the Ethiopian rite. In Ethiopia itself the establishment of any hierarchy has as yet not been possible.

The *Syrians* are the Catholic counterpart of the schismatical Jacobites (Monophysites). They are dispersed throughout Syria and Irak, and some are living outside of Syria. In the United States they number about 7,000. After various attempts at union, a continuity of Catholic allegiance on the part of Syrian Catholics has existed since 1656. Their five residential bishops are headed by the Patriarch of Antioch, whose residence is at Beirut. Those living in the United States are subject to the Latin ordinaries.

The *Maronites* are of Syrian nationality. They live chiefly in the Lebanon. About 38,000 live in the United States, and about 5,000 elsewhere outside their native land. Altogether they number about 366,000. They are without a schismatical counterpart. It is disputed whether they maintained a perpetual orthodoxy, even though it is certain that since 1182 they have been in constant union with Rome. They have eight dioceses and a patriarchal see, which is under the Patriarch of Antioch, whose residence is not fixed in one set place. The Maronites living in the United States are subject to the Latin ordinaries.

The *Malankarese* are the most recent to return to union with Rome. That union was effected in 1930. They received their own hierarchy in 1932, which consists of two residential bishops. Their name was given them to distinguish their rite from the Chaldeo-Malabar rite, originating from the Jacobites of South India. They number about 36,000 faithful.

The *Armenians* fell into schism during the sixth century. Various attempts at union were made, but it was not until 1742 that a union was permanently established. Armenian dioceses exist in Egypt, Palestine, Iran, Syria, and Turkey, subject to the Katholikos of Cilicia, who is the Patriarch of the Catholic Armenians. The Armenians resident in Rumania are under an Apostolic Administrator (since 1930), those living in Galicia have an Archdiocese with its see at Lwòw, and those living in Greece have their respective diocesan see at Athens. These three sees are immediately subject to the Holy See. The Armenians living in the United States are subject to the Latin ordinaries.

The *Chaldeans* were originally Nestorians who lived in Persia and Mesopotamia. Since their union in 1551 the name of Chaldeans was given them lest they should be designated as Catholic Nestorians. Their hierarchy is headed by the Patriarch-Katholikos of Babylon of the Chaldeans, who also is *ex officio* a member of the senate of Irak. They number about 70,000 faithful. There are about 700 Chaldeans in the United States. They have a church in Chicago, St. Ephrem's, subject to the Latin ordinary.

The union of the *Malabarese* with Rome was not effected without many difficulties. Though the union dates from 1599, the Malabarese received their own hierarchy only in 1923. It consists of one archbishop at Ernakulam and three residential bishops. The faithful number about 632,000, all living in India.

There are only very few *Albanians* of the Byzantine rite in union with Rome. Their existence dates from about 1920, when the Archimandrite Germanos at Elbassan with a small group of his people entered into union with Rome.

An early return of the *Bulgarians* to union was foiled by political schemes, so that a union was not procured before 1860. Today only about 6,000 Catholic Bulgarians of the Byzantine rite are left. They are governed by an Apostolic Administrator.

At present there is very little information available about the status of the *Georgians*. Most of them belong to the Orthodox Church, some to the Latin rite, some to the Armenian, and a few to the Byzantine rite.

The *pure Greeks* of the Byzantine rite have been in union with the Holy See since about 1860. Their number is small; about 1,000 belong to the ordinariate of Greece with its see at Athens, and another 1,000 belong to the ordinariate for the Greeks in Turkey with its see at Constantinople.

The *Hungarians* of the Byzantine rite are really a mixture of Ruthenians, Rumanians, and Bulgarians, who in time have become magyarized. In 1912 the diocese of Hajdudorog, as a suffragan of Esztergom, was established for the Hungarians of the Byzantine rite. They number about 142,000 faithful. The great majority of the Hungarians belong to the Latin rite. Those living in the United States belong to the diocese of Pittsburgh (Greek rite).

The *Oriental Catholics of Yugoslavia* are a collection of Ruthenians, Rumanians, Bulgarians, Macedonians, Serbs, and Croations. The latter constitute the greater part of their number. One diocese has been established for these followers of the Byzantine rite at Krizevci, a suffragan see of Zagreb, whose bishop has jurisdiction over all Catholics of the Byzantine rite in Yugoslavia. Those living in the United States belong to the Greek rite diocese of Pittsburgh.

The *Melkites* of Syrian nationality have been in permanent union with Rome since 1724. Today they are spread over Syria, Palestine, Egypt, Turkey, Australia, Mexico, Brazil, and the United States. Altogether they number about 166,000, about 13,000 of this number living in the United States. All Melkites dwelling outside of the old Patriarchates of Antioch, Jerusalem, and Alexandria are subject to the local Latin ordinaries.

After the Turks were driven out of the Danubian basin toward the end of the seventeenth century, the union of the *Rumanians* with Rome was permanently established in 1701. Today there are about 1,500,000 Catholics of the Byzantine rite, and about an equal number of the Latin rite in Rumania. The faithful of the Byzantine rite are divided into five dioceses with a Metropolitan at Fagaras — Alba Julia. In the United States there are about 8,000 Rumanians of the Byzantine rite under the jurisdiction of the Latin ordinaries.

At present it is difficult to give any statistical data on the *Russian Oriental Catholics* of the Byzantine rite. No records are available of the few converts made especially between 1905, when Nicholas II issued an edict of religious tolerance, and 1917, the advent of the bolshevist revolution. Russian communities existed, however, in some of the cities of Europe, such as Paris, Lyons, Lille, Berlin, Vienna, and Prague. In 1928 an ordinariate for the Catholic Russians in China and Manchuria was erected at Harbin. There are about 1,000 Russians of the Byzantine rite in the United States, with communities in New York and Los Angeles.

The Catholics of the Byzantine rite dwelling especially in Galicia, Podcarpathia (Czechoslovakia and Hungary), and Bukovina (Rumania) are known as the *Ruthenians*. Union was formally restored in 1595. They number about 5,000,000 faithful. The Ruthenians in the United States are divided into two dioceses. The Ruthenians from Galicia form the Ukrainian Greek Catholic diocese of Philadelphia, erected in 1913. The Ruthenians of Carpatho-Russian, Hungarian, and Croatian nationalities constitute the diocese of Pittsburgh of the Greek rite. This diocese was erected in 1924, when it was separated from the one of Philadelphia; its Bishop resides at Homestead, Pennsylvania. The total number of Ruthenians in the United States is about 560,000. In Canada a Ruthenian diocese was established at Winnipeg in 1912. It numbers about 300,000 faithful. The Ruthenians in South America are subject to the local Latin ordinaries.

The *Italo-Albanians* have been treated in a more detailed manner in Chapter II, Article 1.

Appendix II

SOURCES FOR THE ORIENTAL CODE

Following is a list of the sources for the Oriental Code as published by the Commission for the Codification of Oriental Law up to 1945.[1]

Fonti, Serie I

Fasc.

I. *Testi vari di diritto nuovo* (1550-1902) — Parte prima (1930).

II. *Testi vari di diritto nuovo* (1550-1902) — Parte seconda (1931).

III. *Disciplina antiochena* (Siri): 1. *Nomocanone di Bar-Hebreo* (1931).

IV. *Disciplina caldea:* I, *Droit ancien: Synodes* (Synodicon orientale): Collectio canonum synodicorum d'Ebedjesus de Nisibe (1931).

V. *Disciplina alessandrina* (Etiopi): Testi di diritto antichi e moderni riguardanti gli Etiopi (1931).

VI. *Disciplina alessandrina:* Testi di diritto antichi riguardanti gli Etiopi (1932).

VII. *Disciplina armena:* Testi vari di diritto canonico armeno (Secoli IV-XVII), (1932).

VIII. *Studi storici sulle fonti di diritto canonico orientale* (1932).

IX. *Disciplina generale antica* (sec. II-IX), (1933).

X. *Disciplina bizantina* (Rumeni): Testi di diritto particolare dei Rumeni (1933).

XI. *Disciplina bizantina* (Ruteni): Testi di diritto particolare dei Ruteni (1933).

XII. *Disciplina antiochena* (Maroniti): Testi di diritto particolare dei Maroniti (1933).

XV. *Discipline byzantine* (Melkites): Droit particulier des Melkites. — Première partie: Textes du droit approuvé (1934).

[1] The writer has added the date of publication for each volume in parentheses. All volumes were published Roma: Typis Polyglottis Vaticanis, except fascicles XII, XXI, XXX of Serie II, which were published Venezia: Tipografia dei Padri Mechitaristi. It is worthy of notice that the third series is called *Fontes,* perhaps in analogy with the *Fontes* of the Code of Canon Law, while the first two series were called *Fonti.*

FONTI, SERIE II

Fasc.

I. *Textes législatifs touchant le cénobitisme égyptien* (1935).

III. *Patriarchatus constantinopolitani acta selecta.* I (1941).

V. *Textus selecti ex operibus commentatorum byzantinorum iuris ecclesiastici* (1939).

VI. *De fontibus iuris ecclesiastici russorum* commentarius historico-canonicus (1936).

VII. *Textus selecti iuris ecclesiastici russorum* (1944).

VIII. *De fontibus iuris ecclesiastici syro-malankarensium,* commentarius historico-canonicus (1937).

IX. *Fontes iuris canonici syro-malankarensium* (1940).

X. *De monachico statu iuxta disciplinam byzantinam,* statuta selectis fontibus et commentariis instructa. Indices (1942).

XII. *Disciplina armena.* Monachismo. Studio storico-canonico e fonti canoniche (1940).

XV. *Caldei. Diritto antico.* II. "*Ordo iudiciorum ecclesiasticorum,*" collectus, dispositus, ordinatus et compositus a Mar 'Abdiso' Metropolita Nisibis et Armeniæ (1940).

XVI. *Caldei. Diritto antico.* III. "*Liber Patrum*" (1940).

XVII. *Caldei. Diritto nuovo.* Les actes du Synode Chaldéen célébré au Convent de Rabban Hormizd près d'Alquoche du 7 au 21 juin 1853. Publiés et annotés par J. M. Vosté O.P. (1942).

XXI. *Disciplina armena. Canones apostolici.* Testo armeno con versione italiana e apparato critico (1941).

XXVII. *Disciplina antiochena* (Siri): Textes concernant les Sacrements (1941).

XXVIII. *Disciplina antiochena* (Siri): Lieux et temps sacrés —Culte divin — Magistère ecclésiastique — Bénéfices et biens temporels ecclésiastiques (1943).

XXX. *Lex textes juridiques dans les Pandectes des Nicon de la Montagne Noire* (1942).

FONTES, SERIES III

Volume

I. *Acta Romanorum Pontificum.* A S. Clemente I (an. c. 90) ad Cœlestinum III (+ 1198).
Tom. I — Introductio, textus actorum, additamentum, appendix (1943).
Tom. II— *Indices* (1943).

II. *Acta Innocenti PP. III* (1944).

VI. *Excerpta ex Actis Synodorum Oecumenicarum* (1944).

CONCLUSIONS

1. The Latin ordinary's jurisdiction over his Oriental subjects is limited by the particular laws of the various Oriental rites concerning the personal status of the Orientals and their liturgy.

2. By virtue of the jurisdiction which the Latin ordinary has over his Oriental subjects, Oriental Catholics subject to the Latin ordinary are bound to the disciplinary laws peculiar to the diocese in which they reside.

3. It is maintained that the Latin ordinary in the United States cannot dispense Oriental Catholics subject to him from those certain impediments which are mentioned in his quinquennial faculties, excepting those impediments of which the power to dispense emanates from the Sacred Congregation of the Holy Office and the Sacred Penitentiary.

4. The fact that the Latin ordinary has Oriental subjects under his jurisdiction does not give him the powers which Oriental law attributes to the office of an Oriental ordinary. Understood are here only those powers inherent in the office of an Oriental ordinary, different from those inherent in the office of a Latin ordinary and peculiar to each Oriental rite.

5. Oriental patriarchs or bishops have no jurisdiction over the faithful of their rite residing in Latin dioceses in the United States.

6. The faculty to permit a transfer from one Oriental rite to another which uses the same kind of bread in the sacrifice of the Mass, as possessed by Oriental bishops according to Oriental law, is still in existence but cannot be used by Latin ordinaries for their Oriental subjects, be-

cause the Latin ordinaries are bound by the provision of canons 98, § 3.

7. It is maintained that canons 44 and 82 of the Code of Canon Law are also applicable to Orientals subject to Latin ordinaries.

BIBLIOGRAPHY

Sources

Acta Apostolica Sedis, Commentarium Officiale, Romæ, 1909-.

Acta et Decreta Concilii Nationalis Armenorum Romæ habiti, an. 1911, Romæ: Typis Polyglottis Vaticanis, 1913.

Acta et Decreta Sacrorum Conciliorum Recentiorum, Collectio Lacensis, 7 vols. Friburgi Brisgoviæ: B. Herder, 1870-1890.

Acta Sanctæ Sedis, 41 vols., Romæ, 1865-1908.

Appendix ad Bullarium Pontificium S. Congregationis de Propaganda Fide, 2 vols., Romæ: Typis Collegii Urbani, [no date given].

Berger, Elie, *Les Registres d'Innocent IV,* 4 vols., Paris: Ernst Thorin, 1884-1897.

Bouscaren, T. Lincoln, *The Canon Law Digest,* 2 vols., Milwaukee, Wis.: The Bruce Publishing Company, 1934-1943.

Bullarium Pontificium Sacræ Congregationis de Propaganda Fide, 7 vols., Romæ: Typis Collegii Urbani, 1839-1858.

Bullarium Diplomatum et Privilegiorum S. R. Pontificum Taurinensis Editio, 20 vols., Augustæ Taurinorum, 1857-1872; 5 vols., Neapoli, 1867-1885.

Codicis Iuris Canonici Fontes cura Emi Petri Card. Gasparri editi, 9 vols., Romæ [postea Civitate Vaticana]: Typis Polyglottis Vaticanis, 1923-1939. (Vols. VII, VIII, et IX ed. cura et studio Emi Iustiniani Card. Seredi.)

Codificazione Canonica Orientale, Fonti, 3 series, Roma: Tipografia Poliglotta Vaticana, 1930-.

Collectanea S. Congregationis de Propaganda Fide, 2 vols., Romæ: Ex Typographia Polyglotta Vaticana, 1907.

Decretales D. Gregorii Papæ IX, una cum Glossis Restitutæ, Romæ, 1582.

Ius Pontificium de Propaganda Fide, ed. R. de Martinis, pars prima: 7 vols. in 8, Romæ, 1888-1897; pars secunda: Romæ, 1909.

Jaffé, Philippus, *Regesta Pontificum Romanorum, ab condita Ecclesia ad annum post Christum natum 1198,* 2 ed., correctam et auctam auspiciis Gulielmi Wattenbach curaverunt S. Loewenfeld, F. Kaltenbrunner, P. Ewald, 2 vol. in 1, Lipsiæ, 1885-1888.

Mansi, J. D., *Sacrorum Conciliorum Nova et Amplissima Collectio,* 53 vols. in 60, Parisiis, 1901-1927.

Mercati, A., *Raccolta di Concordati su Materie ecclesiastiche tra la Santa Sede e le Autorità civili,* Roma: Tipografia Poliglotta Vaticana, 1919.

Potthast, A., *Regesta Pontificum Romanorum inde ab anno post Christum natum 1198 ad annum 1304,* 2 vols., Berolini, 1874-1875.

Pressuti, Petrus I., *Regesta Honorii Papæ III,* 2 vols., Romæ: Ex Typographia Vaticana, 1888-1895.

Synodus Sciarfensis Syrorum in Monte Libano celebrata, an. 1888, Romæ: Typis polygl. S. C. de Prop. Fide. 1896.

Reference Works

Allatius, Leo, *De Aetate et Interstitiis in Collatione Ordinum etiam apud Græcos servandis,* Romæ: Mascardus, 1638.

Attwater, Donald, *The Catholic Eastern Churches,* Milwaukee: The Bruce Publishing Company, 1935.

Augustinus, Antonius, *Antiquæ Decretalium Collectiones Commentariis et Emendationibus Illustratæ. Collectio Quarta Decretalium,* Parisiis, 1621.

Benedictus XIV, *De Synodo Diœcesana,* 2 vols., Romæ, 1767.

Beste, Udalricus, *Introductio in Codicem,* 2 ed., Collegeville, Minn.: St. John's Abbey Press, 1944.

Brehier, Louis, *L'église et l'orient au moyen âge, les croisades,* Paris, 1907.

Cappello, Felix, *Summa Iuris Canonici,* 3 vols., Romæ: Apud Aedes Universitatis Gregorianæ, Vol. I, 2 ed., 1932, 4 ed., 1945; Vol. II, 2 ed., 1934; Vol. III, 1936.

———, *Tractatus Canonico-Moralis de Sacramentis,* 3 vols. in 5, Taurinorum Augustæ: Marietti, 1928-1935.

———, *Tractatus Canonico-Moralis de Censuris,* 2 ed., Taurinorum Augustæ: Marietti, 1925.

Cicognani, Amleto, *Commentarium ad librum I Codicis,* Romæ: ex Schola Typographica "Pio X," 1925.

Coleman, John J., *The Minister of Confirmation,* The Catholic University of America Canon Law Studies, n. 125, Washington, D. C.: The Catholic University of America Press, 1941.

Coussa, Acacius, *Epitome Prælectionum de Iure Ecclesiastico Orientali,* 2 vols., Vol. I: Typis Polyglottis Vaticanis, 1940, Vol. II: Typis Polyglottis Insulæ S. Lazari, 1941.

Dausend, Hugo, *Das interrituelle Recht im Codex Iuris Canonici,* Görres Gesellschaft: Sektion für Rechts- und Staatswissenschaft, n. LXXIX, Paderborn: Verlag Ferdinand Schöningh, 1939.

Dauvillier, Jean-De Clercq, Carlo, *Le Marriage en Droit Canonique Oriental,* Paris: Librarie de Recueil Sirey, 1936.

Duskie, John, *The Canonical Status of the Orientals in the United States,* The Catholic University of America Canon Law Studies, n. 48, Washington, D. C.: The Catholic University of America, 1928.

Eid, Joseph, *A l'Ombre des Cèdres,* privately printed, 1940.

Fortescue, Adrian, *The Lesser Eastern Churches,* London: Catholic Truth Society, 1913.

———, *The Uniate Eastern Churches,* London: Burns Oates & Washbourne, Ltd. 1923.

Gams, Pius Bonifacius, *Series Episcoporum Ecclesiæ Catholicæ,* Ratisbonæ, 1873.

Goodwine, Joseph G., *The Reception of Converts,* The Catholic University of America Canon Law Studies, n. 198, Washington, D. C.: The Catholic University of America Press, 1944.

Hefele, Carolus-Leclercq, Henricus, *Histoire des Conciles,* 10 vols. in 19, Paris: Letouzey et Ané, 1907-1938.

Hergenröther, Joseph, *Handbuch der allgemeinen Kirchengeschichte,* 2 ed., 2 vols., Freiburg im Breisgau: Herder, 1879-1880.

Hostiensis (Henricus de Segusia), *In Quinque Libros Decretalium Commentaria,* 3 vols., Venetiis, 1581.

Ioannes Andreæ, *In Quinque Decretalium Librum Novella Commentaria,* 5 vols., Venetiis, 1581.

Jone, Heribert, *Gesetzbuch des kanonischen Rechtes,* 3 vols., Paderborn: Ferdinand Schöningh, 1939-1940.

Liturgical Arts Society, *The Eastern Branches of the Catholic Church,* New York: Longmans, Green and Co., 1938.

Michiels, Gommarus, *Normæ Generales Iuris Canonici, Commentarium Libri I Iuris Canonici,* 2 vols., Lublin: Universitas Catholica, 1929.

Milasch, N., *Das Kirchenrecht der Morgenländischen Kirche,* translated into German by Dr. Alexander Pessić, Mostar: Pacher & Kisić, 1905.

Nilles, Nicolas, *Symbolæ ad illustrandam historiam ecclesiæ Orientalis in terris Coronæ S. Stephani,* 2 vols. in 1, Oeniponte: F. Rauch, 1885.

Norden, W., *Das Papstum und Byzanz,* Berlin, 1903.

1945 *Official Catholic Directory,* New York: Kenedy & Sons.

Pallen, Condé B., *A Memorial of Andrew J. Shipman, His Life and Writings,* New York: Encyclopedia Press, Inc., 1916.

Papp-Szilágyi, I., *Enchiridion Iuris Ecclesiæ Orientalis Catholicæ,* Magno-Varadini: Typis Eugenii Hollósy, 1880.

Petrani, Alexius, *De Relatione Iuridica inter Diversos Ritus in Ecclesia Catholica,* Romæ: Marietti, 1930.

Schroeder, Henry J., *Disciplinary Decrees of the General Councils,* St. Louis: Herder Book Co., 1937.

Silbernagel, Isidor, *Verfassung und gegenwärtiger Bestand sämtlicher Kirchen des Orients,* 2 ed., by Joseph Schnitzer, Regensburg, 1904.

Statistica con cenni storici della Gerarchia e dei Fedeli di Rito Orientale, Roma: Tipografia Poliglotta Vaticana, 1932.

Ughelli, Ferdinandus, *Italia Sacra, sive de Episcopis Italiæ et insularum adiacentium,* 2 ed., 10 vols., Venice: Sebastian Coleti, 1721.

Van Hove, A., *Commentarium Lovaniense in Codicem Iuris Canonici,* 1 vol. in 5 (Tom. II: *De Legibus Ecclesiasticis,* 1930), Mechlinæ-Romæ: H. Dessain, 1928-1938.

Vering, Friedrich H., *Lehrbuch des katholischen, orientalischen und protestantischen Kirchenrechts,* 3 ed., Freiburg im Breisgau: Herder, 1893.

Vermeersch, Arthurus-Creusen, Josephus, *Epitome Iuris Canonici,* 5 ed., 3 vols., Mechlinæ-Romæ: H. Dessain, 1933-1936.

Wernz, Franciscus-Vidal, Petrus, *Ius Canonicum,* 7 vols. in 8 (Vol. I: *Normæ Generales,* 1938), Romæ: Apud Aedes Universitatis Gregorianæ, 1923-1938.

PERIODICALS

Archiv für katholisches Kirchenrecht, Innsbruck, 1857-1861; Mainz, 1862-.

Bulletin of the Polish Institute of Arts and Sciences in America, New York City, 1943-.

Görres Gesellschaft: Historisches Jahrbuch, Münster, 1880-1882; München, 1883-1930; Köln, 1930-.

Ephemerides Liturgicæ, new series, Romæ, 1927-.

Jurist, The, Washington, D. C., 1941-.

Orientalia Christiana, Romæ, 1923-1934.

Sitzungsberichte der philosophisch-historischen Classe der kaiserlichen Akademie der Wissenschaften, Wien, 1850-1922; Wien und Leipzig, 1923-.

ARTICLES

Arndt, Augustin, "Die gegenseitigen Rechtsverhältnisse der Riten in der katholischen Kirche," — *AKKR,* LXXI (1894), 193-238.

Bastnagel, Clement, "Maronite Law of Abstinence," — *The Jurist,* III (1943), 145-149.

De Clercq, Carolus, "De ritu et adscriptione ritui apud orientales catholicos," — *Ephemerides Liturgicæ*, VI (1932), 473-480.

Fiedler, Joseph, "Beiträge zur Geschichte der Union der Ruthenen in Nordungarn," — *SB*, XXXIX (1862), 481-503.

———, "Die Union der in Ungarn zwischen der Donau wohnenden Bekenner des grieschich-orientalischen Glaubens," — *SB*, XXXVIII (1862), 284-297.

Gillman, Franz, "Der Kommentar des Vincentius Hispanus zu den Kanones des vierten Laterankonzils," — *AKKR*, CIX (1929), 223-274.

Gulovich, Stephen C., "Matrimonial Laws of the Catholic Eastern Churches," — *The Jurist*, IV (1944), 200-245.

———, "The Principle underlying the validity of Oriental marriage law," — *The Jurist*, VI (1946), 39-49.

Herman, Aemilius, "De Ritu in Iure Canonico," — *Orientalia Christiana*, XXXII (1933), 96-158.

———, "Quibus normis matrimonium regatur quod inter fideles diversi ritus contrahitur," — *Analecta Gregoriana*, Vols. IX-X, *Miscellanea Vermeersch*, 2 vols., Roma: Pontificia Università Gregoriana, 1935, I, 241-255.

Hergenröther, Joseph, "Die Rechtsverhältnisse der verschiedenen Riten innerhalb der katholischen Kirche," — *AKKR*, VII (1862), 169-200; 337-363; VIII (1862), 74-97; 161-200.

Pierre, Hieromoine, "L'union de l'Orient avec Rome," — *Orientalia Christiana*, XVIII (1930), 5-156.

Plöchl, Willibald, "The Church Laws for the Orientals of the Austrian Monarchy in 'the Age of Enlightenment,'" — *Polish Institute*, II (1944), 711-756.

———, "Two hundred years 'Etsi pastoralis,'" — *The Jurist*, II (1942), 211-213.

———, "Quinquennial Faculties extended by the S. Congregation for the Oriental Church to Latin Ordinaries," — *The Jurist*, VI (1946), 73-76.

———, "Non-solemn baptism and determination of rite," — *The Jurist*, V (1945), 359-388.

———, "The change of rite 'in matrimonio ineundo vel eo durante,'" — *The Jurist*, VI (1946), 275-304.

Rattinger, D., "Der Patriarchat und Metropolitansprengel von Constantinopel und die bulgarische Kirche zur Zeit der Lateinerherrschaft in Byzanz," — *Görres Gesellschaft: Historisches Jahrbuch*, I (1880), 77-106; II (1881), 31-55.

Abbreviations

AAS — *Acta Apostolicæ Sedis.*

ASS — *Acta Sanctæ Sedis.*

AKKR — *Archiv für katholisches Kirchenrecht.*

Collectanea — *Collectanea S. C. de Propaganda Fide.*

Fontes — *Codicis Iuris Canonici Fontes.*

Fonti — *Codificazione Canonica Orientale, Fonti,* Serie I.

Fonti, Serie II — *Codificazione Canonica Orientale, Fonti,* Serie II.

Polish Institute — *Bulletin of the Polish Institute of Arts and Sciences in America.*

SB — *Sitzungsberichte der philosophisch-historischen Classe der kaiserlichen Akademie der Wissenschaften.*

ALPHABETICAL INDEX

BIOGRAPHICAL NOTE

MICHAEL FERDINAND DIEDERICHS was born October 17, 1916, in Kalenborn, Germany. He there completed all his elementary schooling. In 1930 he entered the Humanistische Studienanstalt Sittard at Sittard, Holland, conducted by the Congregation of the Priests of the Sacred Heart. On October 1, 1936, he entered the novitiate of this Congregation at Sainte Marie, Illinois, making his profession in the following year and becoming a member of the same Congregation. He finished his philosophical and theological studies at the Sacred Heart Monastery, Hales Corners, Wisconsin, in 1943. He was ordained to the Sacred Priesthood on May 30, 1942. In September, 1943, he entered the Catholic University of America for graduate studies in Canon Law. From this University he received the Degree of the Baccalaureate in Canon Law in May, 1944, and the Licentiate in Canon Law in May, 1945.

CANON LAW STUDIES [1]

1. Freriks, Rev. Celestine A., C.PP.S., J.C.D., Religious Congregations in Their External Relations, 121 pp., 1916.
2. Galliher, Rev. Daniel M., O.P., J.C.D., Canonical Elections, 117 pp., 1917.
3. Borkowski, Rev. Aurelius L., O.F.M., J.C.D., De Confraternitatibus Ecclesiasticis, 136 pp., 1918.
4. Castillo, Rev. Cayo, J.C.D., Disertacion Historico-Canonica sobre la Potestad del Cabildo en Sede Vacante o Impedida del Vicario Capitular, 99 pp., 1919 (1918).
5. Kubelbeck, Rev. William J., S.T.B., J.C.D., The Sacred Penitentiaria and Its Relation to Faculties of Ordinaries and Priests, 129 pp., 1918.
6. Petrovits, Rev. Joseph, J. C., S.T.D., J.C.D., The New Church Law on Matrimony, X-461 pp., 1919.
7. Hickey, Rev. John J., S.T.B., J.C.D., Irregularities and Simple Impediments in the New Code of Canon Law, 100 pp., 1920.
8. Klekotka, Rev. Peter J., S.T.B., J.C.D., Diocesan Consultors, 179 pp., 1920.
9. Wanenmacher, Rev. Francis, J.C.D., The Evidence in Ecclesiastical Procedure Affecting the Marriage Bond, 1920 (Printed 1935).
10. Golden, Rev. Henry Francis, J.C.D., Parochial Benefices in the New Code, IV-119 pp., 1921 (Printed 1925).
11. Koudelka, Rev. Charles J., J.C.D., Pastors, Their Rights and Duties According to the New Code of Canon Law, 211 pp., 1921.
12. Melo, Rev. Antonius, O.F.M., J.C.D., De Exemptione Regularium, X-188 pp., 1921.
13. Schaaf, Rev. Valentine Theodore, O.F.M., S.T.B., J.C.D., The Cloister, X-180 pp., 1921.
14. Burke, Rev. Thomas Joseph, S.T.D., J.C.D., Competence in Ecclesiastical Tribunals, IV-117 pp., 1922.
15. Leech, Rev. George Leo, J.C.D., A Comparative Study of the Constitution "Apostolicæ Sedis" and the "Codex Juris Canonici," 179 pp., 1922.

---

[1] Below n. 100 only the following numbers are still available: Nos. 25, 57, and 75. Beginning with n. 100 only the following numbers are unavailable: Nos. 100-111 inclusive, 113 and 115-117 inclusive.

16. MOTRY, REV. HUBERT LOUIS, S.T.D., J.C.D., Diocesan Faculties According to the Code of Canon Law, II-167 pp., 1922.
17. MURPHY, REV. GEORGE LAWRENCE, J.C.D., Delinquencies and Penalties in the Administration and the Reception of the Sacraments, IV-121 pp., 1923.
18. O'REILLY, REV. JOHN ANTHONY, S.T.B., J.C.D., Ecclesiastical Sepulture in the New Code of Canon Law, II-129 pp., 1923.
19. MICHALICKA, REV. WENCESLAS CYRIL, O.S.B., J.C.D., Judicial Procedure in Dismissal of Clerical Exempt Religious, 107 pp., 1923.
20. DARGIN, REV. EDWARD VINCENT, S.T.B., J.C.D., Reserved Cases According to the Code of Canon Law, IV-103 pp., 1924.
21. GODFREY, REV. JOHN A., S.T.B., J.C.D., The Right of Patronage According to the Code of Canon Law, 153 pp., 1924.
22. HAGEDORN, REV. FRANCIS EDWARD, J.C.D., General Legislation on Indulgences, II-154 pp., 1924.
23. KING, REV. JAMES IGNATIUS, J.C.D., The Administration of the Sacraments to Dying Non-Catholics, V-141 pp., 1924.
24. WINSLOW, REV. FRANCIS JOSEPH, O.F.M., J.C.D., Vicars and Prefects Apostolic, IV-149 pp., 1924.
25. CORREA, REV. JOSE SERVELION, S.T.L., J.C.D., La Potestad Legislativa de la Iglesia Catolica, IV-127 pp., 1925.
26. DUGAN, REV. HENRY FRANCIS, A.M., J.C.D., The Judiciary Department of the Diocesan Curia, 87 pp., 1925.
27. KELLER, REV. CHARLES FREDERICK, S.T.B., J.C.D., Mass Stipends, 167 pp., 1925.
28. PASCHANG, REV. JOHN LINUS, J.C.D., The Sacramentals According to the Code of Canon Law, 129 pp., 1925.
29. PIONTEK, REV. CYRILLUS, O.F.M., S.T.B., J.C.D., De Indulto Exclaustrationis necnon Sæcularizationis, XIII-289 pp., 1925.
30. KEARNEY, REV. RICHARD JOSEPH, S.T.B., J.C.D., Sponsors at Baptism According to the Code of Canon Law, IV-127 pp., 1925.
31. BARTLETT, REV. CHESTER JOSEPH, A.M., LL.B., J.C.D., The Tenure of Parochial Property in the United States of America, V-108 pp., 1926.
32. KILKER, REV. ADRIAN JEROME, J.C.D., Extreme Unction, V-425 pp., 1926.
33. MCCORMICK, REV. ROBERT EMMETT, J.C.D., Confessors of Religious, VIII-266 pp., 1926.
34. MILLER, REV. NEWTON THOMAS, J.C.D., Founded Masses According to the Code of Canon Law, VII-93 pp., 1926.

35. ROELKER, REV. EDWARD G., S.T.D., J.C.D., Principles of Privilege According to the Code of Canon Law, XI-166 pp., 1926.
36. BAKALARCZYK, REV. RICHARDUS, M.I.C., J.U.D., De Novitiatu, VIII-208 pp., 1927.
37. PIZZUTI, REV. LAWRENCE, O.F.M., J.U.L., De Parochis Religiosis, 1927. (Not Printed.)
38. BLILEY, REV. NICHOLAS MARTIN, O.S.B., J.C.D., Altars According to the Code of Canon Law, XIX-132 pp., 1927.
39. BROWN, MR. BRENDAN FRANCIS, A.B., LL.M., J.U.D., The Canonical Juristic Personality with Special Reference to its Status in the United States of America, V-212 pp., 1927.
40. CAVANAUGH, REV. WILLIAM THOMAS, C.P., J.U.D., The Reservation of the Blessed Sacrament, VIII-101 pp., 1927.
41. DOHENY, REV. WILLIAM J., C.S.C., A.B., J.U.D., Church Property: Modes of Acquisition, X-118 pp., 1927.
42. FELDHAUS, REV. ALOYSIUS H., C.PP.S., J.C.D., Oratories, IX-141 pp., 1927.
43. KELLY, REV. JAMES PATRICK, A.B., J.C.D., The Jurisdiction of the Simple Confessor, X-208 pp., 1927.
44. NEUBERGER, REV. NICHOLAS J., J.C.D., Canon 6 or the Relation of the Codex Juris Canonici to the Preceding Legislation, V-95 pp., 1927.
45. O'KEEFE, REV. GERALD MICHAEL, J.C.D., Matrimonial Dispensations, Powers of Bishops, Priests, and Confessors, VIII-232 pp., 1927.
46. QUIGLEY, REV. JOSEPH, A. M., A.B., J.C.D., Condemned Societies, 139 pp., 1927.
47. ZAPLOTNIK, REV. JOHANNES LEO, J.C.D., De Vicariis Foraneis, X-142 pp., 1927.
48. DUSKIE, REV. JOHN ALOYSIUS, A.B., J.C.D., The Canonical Status of the Orientals in the United States, VIII-196 pp., 1928.
49. HYLAND, REV. FRANCIS EDWARD, J.C.D., Excommunication, Its Nature, Historical Development and Effects, VIII-181 pp., 1928.
50. REINMANN, REV. GERALD JOSEPH, O.M.C., J.C.D., The Third Order Secular of Saint Francis, 201 pp., 1928.
51. SCHENK, REV. FRANCIS J., J.C.D., The Matrimonial Impediments of Mixed Religion and Disparity of Cult, XVI-318 pp., 1929.
52. COADY, REV. JOHN JOSEPH, S.T.D., J.U.D., A.M., The Appointment of Pastors, VIII-150 pp., 1929.
53. KAY, REV. THOMAS HENRY, J.C.D., Competence in Matrimonial Procedure, VIII-164 pp., 1929.

54. Turner, Rev. Sidney Joseph, C.P., J.U.D., The Vow of Poverty, XLIX-217 pp., 1929.
55. Kearney, Rev. Raymond A., A.B., S.T.D., J.C.D., The Principles of Delegation, VII-149 pp., 1929.
56. Conran, Rev. Edward James, A.B., J.C.D., The Interdict, V-163 pp., 1930.
57. O'Neill, Rev. William H., J.C.D., Papal Rescripts of Favor, VII-218 pp., 1930.
58. Bastnagel, Rev. Clement Vincent, J.U.D., The Appointment of Parochial Adjutants and Assistants, XV-257 pp., 1930.
59. Ferry, Rev. William A., A.B., J.C.D., Stole Fees, V-136 pp., 1930.
60. Costello, Rev. John Michael, A.B., J.C.D., Domicile and Quasi-Domicile, VII-201 pp., 1930.
61. Kremer, Rev. Michael Nicholas, A.B., S.T.B., J.C.D., Church Support in the United States, VI-136 pp., 1930.
62. Angulo, Rev. Luis, C.M., J.C.D., Legislation de la Iglesia sobre la intencion en la application de la Santa Misa, VII-104 pp., 1931.
63. Frey, Rev. Wolfgang Norbert, O.S.B., A.B., J.C.D., The Act of Religious Profession, VIII-174 pp. 1931.
64. Roberts, Rev. James Brendan, A.B., J.C.D., The Banns of Marriage, XIV-140 pp., 1931.
65. Ryder, Rev. Raymond Aloysius, A.B., J.C.D., Simony, IX-151 pp., 1931.
66. Campagna, Rev. Angelo, Ph.D., J.U.D., Il Vicario Generale del Vescovo, VII-205 pp., 1931.
67. Cox, Rev. Joseph Godfrey, A.B., J.C.D., The Administration of Seminaries, VI-124 pp., 1931.
68. Gregory, Rev. Donald J., J.U.D., The Pauline Privilege, XV-165 pp., 1931.
69. Donohue, Rev. John F., J.C.D., The Impediment of Crime, VII-110 pp., 1931.
70. Dooley, Rev. Eugene A., O.M.I., J.C.D., Church Law on Sacred Relics, IX-143 pp., 1931.
71. Orth, Rev. Clement Raymond, O.M.C., J.C.D., The Approbation of Religious Institutes, 171 pp., 1931.
72. Pernicone, Rev. Joseph M., A.B., J.C.D., The Ecclesiastical Prohibition of Books, XII-267 pp., 1932.
73. Clinton, Rev. Connell, A.B., J.C.D., The Paschal Precept, IX-108 pp., 1932.

74. Donnelly, Rev. Francis B., A.M., S.T.L., J.C.D., The Diocesan Synod, VIII-125 pp., 1932.
75. Torrente, Rev. Camilo, C.M.F., Las Procesiones Sagradas, V-145 pp., 1932.
76. Murphy, Rev. Edwin J., C.PP.S., J.C.D., Suspension Ex Informata Conscientia, XI-122 pp., 1932.
77. MacKenzie, Rev. Eric F., A.M., S.T.L., J.C.D., The Delict of Heresy in its Commission, Penalization, Absolution, VII-124 pp., 1932.
78. Lyons, Rev. Avitus E., S.T.B., J.C.D., The Collegiate Tribunal of First Instance, XI-147 pp., 1932.
79. Connolly, Rev. Thomas A., J.C.D., Appeals, XI-195 pp., 1932.
80. Sangmeister, Rev. Joseph V., A.B., J.C.D., Force and Fear as Precluding Matrimonial Consent, V-211 pp., 1932.
81. Jaeger, Rev. Leo A., A.B., J.C.D., The Administration of Vacant and Quasi-Vacant Episcopal Sees in the United States, IX-229 pp., 1932.
82. Rimlinger, Rev. Herbert T., J.C.D., Error Invalidating Matrimonial Consent, VII-79 pp., 1932.
83. Barrett, Rev. John D. M., S.S., J.C.D., A Comparative Study of the Third Plenary Council of Baltimore and the Code, IX-221 pp., 1932.
84. Carberry, Rev. John J., Ph.D., S.T.D., J.C.D., The Juridical Form of Marriage, X-177 pp., 1934.
85. Dolan, Rev. John L., A.B., J.C.D., The Defensor Vinculi, XII-157 pp., 1934.
86. Hannan, Rev. Jerome D., A.M., S.T.D., LL.B., J.C.D., The Canon Law of Wills, IX-517 pp., 1934.
87. Lemieux, Rev. Delise A., A.M., J.C.D., The Sentence in Ecclesiastical Procedure, IX-131 pp., 1934.
88. O'Rourke, Rev. James J., A.B., J.C.D., Parish Registers, VII-109 pp., 1934.
89. Timlin, Rev. Bartholomew, O.F.M., A.M., J.C.D., Conditional Matrimonial Consent, X-381 pp., 1934.
90. Wahl, Rev. Francis X., A.B., J.C.D., The Matrimonial Impediments of Consanguinity and Affinity, VI-125 pp., 1934.
91. White, Rev. Robert J., A.B., LL.B., S.T.B., J.C.D., Canonical Ante-Nuptial Promises and the Civil Law, VI-152 pp., 1934.
92. Herrera, Rev. Antonio Parra, O.C.D., J.C.D., Legislacion Eclesiastica sobra el Ayuno y la Abstinencia, XI-191 pp., 1935.

93. KENNEDY, REV. EDWIN J., J.C.D., The Special Matrimonial Process in Cases of Evident Nullity, X-165 pp., 1935.
94. MANNING, REV. JOHN J., A.B., J.C.D., Presumption of Law in Matrimonial Procedure, XI-111 pp., 1935.
95. MOEDER, REV. JOHN M., J.C.D., The Proper Bishop for Ordination and Dimissorial Letters, VII-135 pp., 1935.
96. O'MARA, REV. WILLIAM A., A.B., J.C.D., Canonical Causes for Matrimonial Dispensations, IX-155 pp., 1935.
97. REILLY, REV. PETER, J.C.D., Residence of Pastors, IX-81 pp., 1935.
98. SMITH, REV. MARINER T., O.P., S.T.LR., J.C.D., The Penal Law for Religious, VII-169 pp., 1935.
99. WHALEN, REV. DONALD W., A.M., J.C.D., The Value of Testimonial Evidence in Matrimonial Procedure, XIII-297 pp., 1935.
100. CLEARY, REV. JOSEPH F., J.C.D., Canonical Limitations on the Alienation of Church Property, VIII-141 pp., 1936.
101. GLYNN, REV. JOHN C., J.C.D., The Promoter of Justice, XX-337 pp., 1936.
102. BRENNAN, REV. JAMES H., S.S., M.A., S.T.B., J.C.D., The Simple Convalidation of Marriage, VI-135 pp., 1937.
103. BRUNINI, REV. JOSEPH BERNARD, J.C.D., The Clerical Obligations of Canons 139 and 142, X-121 pp., 1937.
104. CONNOR, REV. MAURICE, A.B., J.C.D., The Administrative Removal of Pastors, VIII-159 pp., 1937.
105. GUILFOYLE, REV. MERLIN JOSEPH, J.C.D., Custom, XI-144 pp., 1937.
106. HUGHES, REV. JAMES AUSTIN, A.B., A.M., J.C.D., Witnesses in Criminal Trials of Clerics, IX-140 pp., 1937.
107. JANSEN, REV. RAYMOND J., A.B., S.T.L., J.C.D., Canonical Provisions for Catechetical Instruction, VII-153 pp., 1937.
108. KEALY, REV. JOHN JAMES, A.B., J.C.D., The Introductory Libellus in Church Court Procedure, XI-121 pp., 1937.
109. McMANUS, REV. JAMES EDWARD, C.SS.R., J.C.D., The Administration of Temporal Goods in Religious Institutes, XVI-196 pp., 1937.
110. MORIARTY, REV. EUGENE JAMES, J.C.D., Oaths in Ecclesiastical Courts, X-115 pp., 1937.
111. RAINER, REV. ELIGIUS GEORGE, C.SS.R., J.C.D., Suspension of Clerics, XVII-249 pp., 1937.
112. REILLY, REV. THOMAS F., C.SS.R., J.C.D., Visitation of Religious, VI-195 pp., 1938.

113. Moriarty, Rev. Francis E., C.SS.R., J.C.D., The Extraordinary Absolution from Censures, XV-334 pp., 1938.
114. Connolly, Rev. Nicholas P., J.C.D., The Canonical Erection of Parishes, X-132 pp., 1938.
115. Donovan, Rev. James Joseph, J.C.D., The Pastor's Obligation in Prenuptial Investigation, XII-322 pp., 1938.
116. Harrigan, Rev. Robert J., M.A., S.T.B., J.C.D., The Radical Sanation of Invalid Marriages, VIII-208 pp., 1938.
117. Boffa, Rev. Conrad Humbert, J.C.D., Canonical Provisions for Catholic Schools, VII-211 pp., 1939.
118. Parsons, Rev. Anscar John, O.M.Cap., J.C.D., Canonical Elections, XII-236 pp., 1939.
119. Reilly, Rev. Edward Michael, A.B., J.C.D., The General Norms of Dispensation, XII-156 pp., 1939.
120. Ryan, Rev. Gerald Aloysius, A.B., J.C.D., Principles of Episcopal Jurisdiction, XII-172 pp., 1939.
121. Burton, Rev. Francis James, C.S.C., A.B., J.C.D., A Commentary on Canon 1125, X-222 pp., 1940.
122. Miaskiewicz, Rev. Francis Sigismund, J.C.D., Supplied Jurisdiction According to Canon 209, XII-340 pp., 1940.
123. Rice, Rev. Patrick William, A.B., J.C.D., Proof of Death in Prenuptial Investigation, VIII-156 pp., 1940.
124. Anglin, Rev. Thomas Francis, M.S., J.C.D., The Eucharistic Fast, VIII-183 pp., 1941.
125. Coleman, Rev. John Jerome, J.C.D., The Minister of Confirmation, VI-153 pp., 1941.
126. Downs, Rev. Joseph Emmanuel, A.B., J.C.D., The Concept of Clerical Immunity, XI-163 pp., 1941.
127. Esswein, Rev. Anthony Albert, J.C.D., Extrajudicial Penal Powers of Ecclesiastical Superiors, X-144 pp., 1941.
128. Farrell, Rev. Benjamin Francis, M.A., S.T.L., J.C.D., The Rights and Duties of the Local Ordinary Regarding Congregations of Women Religious of Pontifical Approval, V-195 pp., 1941.
129. Feeney, Rev. Thomas John, A.B., S.T.L., J.C.D., Restitutio in Integrum, VI-169 pp., 1941.
130. Findlay, Rev. Stephen William, O.S.B., A.B., J.C.D., Canonical Norms Governing the Deposition and Degradation of Clerics, XVII-279 pp., 1941.
131. Goodwine, Rev. John, A.B., S.T.L., J.C.D., The Right of the Church to Acquire Property, VIII-119 pp., 1941.

132. HESTON, REV. EDWARD LOUIS, C.S.C., PH.D., S.T.D., J.C.D., The Alienation of Church Property in the United States, XII-222 pp., 1941.
133. HOGAN, REV. JAMES JOHN, A.B., S.T.L., J.C.D., Judicial Advocates and Procurators, XII-200 pp., 1941.
134. KEALY, REV. THOMAS M., A.B., LITT.B., J.C.D., Dowry of Women Religious, IX-152 pp., 1941.
135. KEENE, REV. MICHAEL JAMES, O.S.B., J.C.D., Religious Ordinaries and Canon 198, V-164 pp., 1942.
136. KERIN, REV. CHARLES A., S.S., M.A., S.T.B., J.C.D., The Privation of Christian Burial, XVI-279 pp., 1941.
137. LOUIS, REV. WILLIAM FRANCIS, M.A., J.C.D., Diocesan Archives, X-101 pp., 1941.
138. MCDEVITT, REV. GILBERT JOSEPH, A.B., J.C.D., Legitimacy and Legitimation, X-247 pp., 1941.
139. MCDONOUGH, REV. THOMAS JOSEPH, A.B., J.C.D., Apostolic Administrators, X-217 pp., 1941.
140. MEIER, REV. CARL ANTHONY, A.B., J.C.D., Penal Administration Procedure Against Negligent Pastors, XI-240 pp., 1941.
141. SCHMIDT, REV. JOHN ROGG, A.B., J.C.D., The Principles of Authentic Interpretation in Canon 17 of the Code of Canon Law, XII-331 pp., 1941.
142. SLAFKOSKY, REV. ANDREW LEONARD, A.B., J.C.D., The Canonical Episcopal Visitation of the Diocese, X-197 pp., 1941.
143. SWOBODA, REV. INNOCENT ROBERT, O.F.M., J.C.D., Ignorance in Relation to the Imputability of Delicts, IX-271 pp., 1941.
144. DUBE, REV. ARTHUR JOSEPH, A.B., J.C.D., The General Principles for the Reckoning of Time in Canon Law, VIII-299 pp., 1941.
145. MCBRIDE, REV. JAMES T., A.B., J.C.D., Incardination and Excardination of Seculars, XX-585 pp., 1941.
146. KROL, REV. JOHN T., J.C.D., The Defendant in Ecclesiastical Trials, XII-207 pp., 1942.
147. COMYNS, REV. JOSEPH J., C.SS.R., A.B., J.C.D., Papal and Episcopal Administration of Church Property, XIV-155 pp., 1942.
148. BARRY, REV. GARRET FRANCIS, O.M.I., J.C.D., Violation of the Cloister, XII-260 pp., 1942.
149. BOLDUC, REV. GATIEN, C.S.V., A.B., S.T.L., J.C.D., Les Etudes dans les Religions Clericales, VII-155 pp., 1942.
150. BOYLE, REV. DAVID JOHN, M.A., J.C.D., The Juridic Effects of Moral Certitude on Pre-Nuptial Guarantees, XII-188 pp., 1942.

151. CANAVAN, REV. WALTER JOSEPH, M.A., LITT.D., J.C.D., The Profession of Faith, XII-143 pp., 1942.
152. DESROCHERS, REV. BRUNO, A.B., PH.L., S.T.B., J.C.D., Le Premier Concile Plenier de Quebec et le Code de Drôit Canonique, XIV-186 pp., 1942.
153. DILLON, REV. ROBERT EDWARD, A.B., J.C.D., Common Law Marriage, X-148 pp., 1942.
154. DODWELL, REV. EDWARD JOHN, PH.D., S.T.B., J.C.D., The Time and Place for the Celebration of Marriage, X-156 pp., 1942.
155. DONNELLAN, REV. THOMAS ANDREW, A.B., J.C.D., The Obligation of the Missa pro Populo, VII-131 pp., 1942.
156. ELTZ, REV. LOUIS ANTHONY, A.B., J.C.D., Coöperation in Crime, XII-208 pp., 1942.
157. GASS, REV. SYLVESTER FRANCIS, M.A., J.C.D., Ecclesiastical Pensions, XI-206 pp., 1942.
158. GUINIVEN, REV. JOHN JOSEPH, C.SS.R., J.C.D., The Precept of Hearing Mass, XIV-188 pp., 1942.
159. GULCZYNSKI, REV. JOHN THEOPHILUS, J.C.D., The Desecration and Violation of Churches, X-126 pp., 1942.
160. HAMMILL, REV. JOHN LEO, M.A., J.C.D., The Obligations of the Traveler According to Canon 14, VIII-204 pp., 1942.
161. HAYDT, REV. JOHN JOSEPH, A.B., J.C.D., Reserved Benefices, XI-148 pp., 1942.
162. HUSER, REV. ROGER JOHN, O.F.M., A.B., J.C.D., The Crime of Abortion in Canon Law, XII-187 pp., 1942.
163. KEARNEY, REV. FRANCIS PATRICK, A.B., S.T.L., J.C.L., The Principles of Canon 1127.
164. LINAHEN, REV. LEO JAMES, S.T.L., J.C.D., De Absolutione Complicis In Peccato Turpi, 114 pp., 1942.
165. MCCLOSKEY, REV. JOSEPH ALOYSIUS, A.B., J.C.D., The Subject of Ecclesiastical Law According to Canon 12, XVII-246 pp., 1942.
166. O'NEILL, REV. FRANCIS JOSEPH, C.SS.R., J.C.D., The Dismissal of Religious in Temporary Vows, XIII-220 pp., 1942.
167. PRINCE, REV. JOHN EDWARD, A.B., S.T.D., J.C.D., The Diocesan Chancellor, X-136 pp., 1942.
168. RIESNER, REV. ALBERT JOSEPH, C.SS.R., J.C.D., Apostates and Fugitives from Religious Institutes, IX-168 pp., 1942.
169. STENGER, REV. JOSEPH BERNARD, J.C.D., The Mortgaging of Church Property, 186 pp., 1942.

170. WALDRON, REV. JOSEPH FRANCIS, A.B., J.C.D., The Minister of Baptism, XII-197 pp., 1942.
171. WILLETT, REV. ROBERT ALBERT, J.C.D., The Probative Value of Documents in Ecclesiastical Trials, X-124 pp., 1942.
172. WOEBER, REV. EDWARD MARTIN, M.A., J.C.D., The Interpellations, XII-161 pp., 1942.
173. BENKO, REV. MATTHEW ALOYSIUS, O.S.B., M.A., J.C.D., The Abbot *Nullius,* XIV-148 pp., 1943.
174. CHRIST, REV. JOSEPH JAMES, M.A., S.T.L., J.C.D., Dispensation from Vindicative Penalties, XIV-285 pp., 1943.
175. CLANCY, REV. PATRICK M. J., O.P., A.B., S.T.LR., J.C.D., The Local Religious Superior, X-229 pp., 1943.
176. CLARKE, REV. THOMAS JAMES, J.C.D., Parish Societies, XII-147 pp., 1943.
177. CONNOLLY, REV. JOHN PATRICK, S.T.L., J.C.D., Synodal Examiners and Parish Priest Consultors, X-223 pp., 1943.
178. DRUMM, REV. WILLIAM MARTIN, A.B., J.C.D., Hospital Chaplains, XII-175 pp., 1943.
179. FLANAGAN, REV. BERNARD JOSEPH, A.B., S.T.L., J.C.D., The Canonical Erection of Religious Houses, X-147 pp., 1943.
180. KELLEHER, REV. STEPHEN JOSEPH, A.B., S.T.B., J.C.D., Discussions with non-Catholics: Canonical Legislation, X-93 pp., 1943.
181. LEWIS, REV. GORDIAN, C.P., J.C.D., Chapters in Religious Institutes, XII-169 pp., 1943.
182. MARX, REV. ADOLPH, J.C.D., The Declaration of Nullity of Marriages Contracted Outside the Church, X-151 pp., 1943.
183. MATULENAS, REV. RAYMOND ANTHONY, O.S.B., A.B., J.C.L., Communication, a Source of Privileges, XII-225 pp., 1943.
184. O'LEARY, REV. CHARLES GERARD, C.SS.R., J.C.D., Religious Dismissed After Perpetual Profession, X-213 pp., 1943.
185. POWER, REV. CORNELIUS MICHAEL, J.C.D., The Blessing of Cemeteries, XII-231 pp., 1943.
186. SHUHLER, REV. RALPH VINCENT, O.S.A., J.C.D., Privileges of Regulars to Absolve and Dispense, XII-195 pp., 1943.
187. ZIOLKOWSKI, REV. THADDEUS STANISLAUS, A.B., J.C.D., The Consecration and Blessing of Churches, XII-151 pp., 1943.
188. HENEGHAN, REV. JOHN JOSEPH, S.T.D., J.C.D., The Marriages of Unworthy Catholics: Canons 1065 and 1066, XVI-213 pp., 1944.

189. Carroll, Rev. Coleman Francis, M.A., S.T.L., J.C.L., Charitable Institutions.
190. Ciesluk, Rev. Joseph Edward, Ph.B., S.T.L., J.C.L., National Parishes in the United States.
191. Coburn, Rev. Vincent Paul, A.B., J.C.D., Marriages of Conscience, XII-172 pp., 1944.
192. Connors, Rev. Charles Paul, C.S.Sp., A.B., J.C.L., Extra-Judicial Procurators in the Code of Canon Law, X-94 pp., 1944.
193. Coyle, Rev. Paul Raymond, A.B., J.C.L., Judicial Exceptions.
194. Fair, Rev. Bartholomew Francis, A.B., S.T.L., J.C.L., The Impediment of Abduction.
195. Gallagher, Rev. Thomas Raphael, O.P., A.B., S.T.Lr., J.C.L., The Examination of the Qualities of the Ordinand, X-166 pp., 1944.
196. Gannon, Rev. John Mark, S.T.L., J.C.L., The Interstices Required for the Promotion to Orders, XII-100 pp., 1944.
197. Goldsmith, Rev. J. William, B.C.S., S.T.L., J.C.L., The Competence of Church and State over Marriage — Disputed Points, X-128 pp., 1944.
198. Goodwine, Rev. Joseph Gerard, A.B., S.T.B., J.C.L., The Reception of Converts, XIV-326 pp., 1944.
199. Kowalski, Rev. Romuald Eugene, O.F.M., A.B., J.C.D., Sustenance of Religious Houses of Regulars, X-174 pp., 1944.
200. McCoy, Rev. Alan Edward, O.F.M., J.C.D., Force and Fear in Relation to Delictual Imputability and Penal Responsibility, XII-160 pp., 1944.
201. McDevitt, Rev. Vincent John, Jh.B., S.T.L., J.C.L., Perjury.
202. Martin, Rev. Thomas Owen, Ph.D., S.T.D., J.C.D., Adverse Possession, Prescription and Limitation of Actions: The Canonical "Præscriptio," XX-208 pp., 1944.
203. Miklosovic, Rev. Paul John, A.B., J.C.L., Attempted Marriages and Their Consequent Juridic Effects.
204. Mundy, Rev. Thomas Maurice, A.B., S.T.L., J.C.L., The Union of Parishes.
205. O'Dea, Rev. John Coyle, A.B., J.C.D., The Matrimonial Impediment of Nonage, VIII-126 pp., 1944.
206. Olalia, Rev. Alexander Ayson, S.T.L., J.C.D., A Comparative Study of the Christian Constitution of States and the Constitution of the Philippine Commonwealth, XII-136 pp., 1944.

207. Poisson, Rev. Pierre-Marie, C.S.C., A.B., Ph.L., J.C.L., Droits Patrimoniaux des Maisons et des Eglises Religieuses.
208. Stadalnikas, Rev. Casimir Joseph, M.I.C., J.C.D., Reservation of Censures, X-141 pp., 1944.
209. Sullivan, Rev. Eugene Henry, S.T.L., J.C.D., Proof of the Reception of the Sacraments, X-165 pp., 1944.
210. Vaughan, Rev. William Edward, J.C.D., Constitutions for Diocesan Courts, X-210 pp., 1944.
211. Paro, Rev. Gino, S.T.D., J.C.L., The Right of Apostolic Delegation.
212. Balzer, Rev. Ralph Francis, C.P., J.C.L., The Computation of Time in a Canonical Novitiate.
213. Dougherty, Rev. John Whelan, A.B., S.T.L., J.C.L., De Inquisitione Speciali.
214. Dziob, Rev. Michael Walter, J.C.L., The Sacred Congregation for the Oriental Church.
215. Eidenschink, Rev. John Albert, O.S.B., B.A., J.C.L., The Election of Bishops in the Letters of Pope Gregory the Great.
216. Gill, Rev. Nicholas, C.P., J.C.L., The Spiritual Prefect in Clerical Religious Houses of Study.
217. Hynes, Rev. Harry Gerard, S.T.L., J.C.L., The Privileges of Cardinals.
218. McDevitt, Rev. Gerard Vincent, S.T.L., J.C.D., The Renunciation of an Ecclesiastical Office, XIV-179 pp., 1945.
219. Manning, Rev. Joseph Leroy, J.C.L., The Free Conferral of Offices.
220. Meyer, Rev. Louis G., O.S.B., A.B., S.T.B., J.C.D., Alms-Gathering by Religious, XII-163 pp., 1945.
221. O'Donnell, Rev. Cletus Francis, M.A., J.C.L., The Marriage of Minors.
222. Prunskis, Rev. Joseph, J.C.D., Comparative Law, Ecclesiastical and Civil, in Lithuanian Concordat, X-161, pp., 1945.
223. Sweeney, Rev. Francis Patrick, C.SS.R., J.C.D., The Reduction of Clerics to the Lay State, X-199 pp., 1945.
224. Vogelpohl, Rev. Henry John, J.C.L., The Simple Impediments to Holy Orders.
225. Brockhaus, Rev. Thomas G., O.S.B., J.C.L., Religious Who Are Known as Conversi.
226. Griese, Rev. N. Orville, S.T.D., J.C.L., Marriage and Procreation of Offspring.

227. BOUDREAUX, REV. WARREN LOUIS, J.C.L., The "ab acatholicis nati" of Canon 1099, 2.
228. BOWE, REV. THOMAS JOSEPH, A.B., J.C.L., Religious Superioresses.
229. DIEDERICHS, REV. MICHAEL FERDINAND, S.C.J., J.C.L., The Jurisdiction of the Latin Ordinaries Over Their Oriental Subjects.
230. DINGMAN, REV. MAURICE JOHN, A.B., S.T.L., J.C.L., The Plaintiff in Contentious Trials.
231. FRISON, REV. BASIL M., C.M.F., M.MUS., J.C.L., The Retroactivity of Law.
232. GALVIN, REV. WILLIAM ANTHONY, M.A., J.C.L., The Administrative Transfer of Pastors.
233. GORACY, REV. JOSEPH C., J.C.L., The Diriment Matrimonial Impediment of Major Orders.
234. HALE, REV. JOSEPH FRANCIS, M.A., S.T.L., J.C.L., The Pastor of Burial.
235. HENRY, REV. JOSEPH, A.B., J.C.L., The Mass and Holy Communion: Interritual Law.
236. LINENBERGER, REV. HERBERT, C.PP.S., J.C.L., Falsa Delatio (Can. 893 and 2363).
237. LOWRY, REV. JAMES MARTIN, B.A., J.C.L., Dispensation from Private Vows.
238. LYNCH, REV. GEORGE EDWARD, A.B., S.T.L., J.C.L., Coadjutors and Auxiliaries of Bishops.
239. LYNCH, REV. TIMOTHY, M.S.SS.T., J.C.L., Contracts Between Bishops and Religious Congregations.
240. MCCLUNN, REV. JUSTIN DAVID, A.B., S.T.L., J.C.L., Administrative Recourse.
241. MCGARVEY, REV. THOMAS JOSEPH, A.B., S.T.L., J.C.L., Bination.
242. MCGRATH, REV. JAMES, A.B., J.C.L., The Privilege of the Canon.
243. MARBACH, REV. JOSEPH FRANCIS, A.B., J.C.L., Marriage Legislation for the Catholics of the Oriental Rites in the United States and Canada.
244. SHIMKUS, REV. BERNARD ALOYSIUS, A.B., J.C.L., The Determination and Transfer of Rite.
245. SMITH, REV. VINCENT M., S.T.L., J.C.L., Ignorance Affecting Matrimonial Consent.
246. WACHTRLE, REV. PAUL ANTHONY, A.B., J.C.L., The Baptism of the Children of Non-Catholics.

www.ingramcontent.com/pod-product-compliance
Lightning Source LLC
LaVergne TN
LVHW050226080826
844660LV00012B/475

* 9 7 8 0 8 1 3 2 2 4 1 3 8 *